LEGACY

WHAT THE ALL BLACKS
CAN TEACH US ABOUT THE
BUSINESS OF LIFE

LEGACY

15 LESSONS IN LEADERSHIP

JAMES KERR

Constable · London

CONSTABLE

First published in Great Britain in 2013 by Constable, an imprint of Constable
& Robinson Ltd. This edition published in 2015 by Constable

5 7 9 8 6 4

A CIP catalogue record for this book
is available from the British Library.

ISBN 978-1-4721-0353-6

Printed and bound in Great Britain by CPI Group (UK) Ltd,Croydon CR0 4YY

Papers used by Constable are from well-managed forests and
other responsible sources

MIX
Paper from
responsible sources
FSC
www.fsc.org   FSC® C104740

Constable is an imprint of Little, Brown Book Group.
Carmelite House, 50 Victoria Embankment, London EC4Y 0DZ

An Hachette UK Company
www.hachette.co.uk

www.littlebrown.co.uk

The Challenge

When the opposition line up against the New Zealand national rugby team – the All Blacks – they face the *haka*, the highly ritualized challenge thrown down by one group of warriors to another. Māori believe that the *haka* draws up *tīpuna*, our ancestors, from the earth to the soul. It summons them to aid us in our struggle here on earth with the sound of *ngunguru*, the low rumble of an earthquake:

> _____ *'Tis death! 'tis death!*
>   *I may die! I may die!*
>   *'Tis life! 'tis life!*
>   *I might live! I might live!*

Opposing teams face the *haka* in different ways. Some try to ignore it, others advance on it, most stand shoulder to shoulder to face it. Whatever their outward response, inwardly the opposition know that they are standing before more than a collection of fifteen individual players. They are facing a culture, an identity, an ethos, a belief system – and a collective passion and purpose beyond anything they have faced before.

Often, by the time the *haka* reaches its crescendo, the opposition have already lost. For rugby, like business and like much of life, is played primarily in the mind.

The All Blacks are the most successful rugby team in history. They have been called the most successful sports team, in any code, ever. In the professional era, they have an extraordinary win rate of over 86 per cent and are the current World Champions.

How do the All Blacks do it?

What's the secret of their success?

What is their competitive advantage?

And what can we learn from it?

~

In June 2010, alongside photojournalist Nick Danziger, I was embedded for five weeks inside the All Blacks set-up as they began working towards the Rugby World Cup. This gave me a privileged insight into an extraordinary high-performance culture; I learnt that their methods provide an inspiring and effective model for leaders in other fields.

In February 2013, I revisited former team coach Sir Graham Henry and his right-hand men Wayne Smith and Gilbert Enoka, key figures in the All Blacks' World Cup success, and asked them some questions of leadership. I also spoke to iconic former All Blacks, advertising men, management consultants, HR and engagement specialists, designers, teachers, lawyers, a cocktail of psychiatrists, psychologists and physiotherapists, an opera singer, a stunt pilot and experts in Māori tribal customs, language and beliefs. I cross-referenced the research to my own experience in brand storytelling, culture change and engagement for some of the world's leading businesses in an attempt to explain the All Blacks' exceptional success and how we might apply it to leading our own businesses and our own lives.

What I learnt forms the basis of this book.

~

The *haka* reminds us of the inherent fragility of all life. How little time is given to each of us. And how much we still have to do.

It reminds us:

This is our time.

James Kerr

CONTENTS

Exceptional success requires exceptional circumstances.
Wayne Smith, former All Blacks assistant coach

I

CHARACTER

———— *Waiho mā te tangata e mihi.*
Let someone else praise your virtues.

SWEEP THE SHEDS
Never be too big to do
the small things that
need to be done

New Zealand v Wales, Carisbrook, Dunedin, 19 June 2010

'It's a cold place, Carisbrook,' says All Blacks centre Conrad Smith. 'The wind whips off Antarctica and heads straight for your balls.' The posters for the match say 'Welcome to the House of Pain'.

Head coach Graham Henry takes a walk with Raewyn, his wife – a pre-match ritual. His assistants, Wayne Smith and Steve Hansen, chat with manager Darren Shand in the breakfast room of the hotel. Gilbert Enoka, the mental skills coach, moves through the players, chatting. Their barefoot guru.

Upstairs, Errol Collins, aka 'Possum', the baggage man, begins laying out the jerseys.

Every team has its Poss. Ostensibly his role is to take care of the kit. From goal pads to practise balls, warm-up jackets to chewing gum, training socks to sensible, wry, homespun advice, Poss is your man. He's there to take care of the players. On test day, he lays out the black jersey.

Māori have a word, *taonga*, which means treasure. The black jersey is *taonga*, a sacred object.

This black jersey with its silver fern.

Since 1905, when the 'Originals' arrived and took Europe by storm, the black jersey has captured the essence and hopes of this small island nation. Over the last 100 years or so it has transformed from a makeshift garment with laces at the neck to the modern, sweat-wicking, tight-fitting gladiatorial armour of today, but at heart it remains the same; a symbol of excellence, hard work and a New Zealander's ability to become, with effort, sacrifice and skill, the best in the world.

> Successful leaders balance pride with humility: absolute pride in performance; total humility before the magnitude of the task.

After an early lunch – chicken, baked potatoes – the players head upstairs in twos and threes: the captain, Richie McCaw, Kieran Read, Tony Woodcock, Brad Thorn, Joe Rokocoko . . . The Chosen.

They collect their prize: black shorts, black socks with three white stripes, the black jersey with the silver fern. As the jerseys go on, so do the 'game faces'. The players become All Blacks.

'I can still remember Richie McCaw's first jersey,' Gilbert Enoka says. 'He spent about forty-five seconds to a minute with his head just buried in the jersey.'

Today is McCaw's ninety-first test.

~

'A win today against the Welsh is not enough,' says a pundit. 'It has to be a big win.'

In the stadium, beer cans rattle against the hoardings. A helicopter thumps overhead. Someone sells T-shirts.

McCaw steps off the bus. There is a cry, a *pōwhiri*, the traditional Māori welcome. A lone Māori male with a *taiaha*, a thrusting spear. There is an explosion of camera flashes.

McCaw accepts the challenge on behalf of the team.

Women swoon. Men too.

The All Blacks head for the sheds.

Under the stadium there are trestle tables loaded with lineaments, bandages, and cups of carbohydrates. The New Zealand flag is on the wall; the Union Jack and the Southern Cross.

There are no histrionics. The team prepares silently, many in headphones. Above, 35,000 voices chant, 'Black! Black! Black!'

The coaches hang back as the players prepare. There is no rousing rhetoric. A word here, a backslap there. Now it is all about the players. About 'the being of team'.

The talking is done. It's time to play rugby.

~

It turns out to be Dan Carter's day, one of his finest. The New Zealand playmaker runs in two tries, the second of which will be replayed for as long as the game is loved. He scores 27 points, the Perfect Ten. Later, the papers will say 'the Welsh have no answers'.

The All Blacks win, 42-7.

Carter has proved himself, once again, indispensible. But, really, it's Richie McCaw's time. Today he becomes statistically the most successful All Blacks captain ever.

~

In the sheds, the drink flows.

The room fills with journalists, politicians, sponsors, their sons, their sons' best friends. Dr Deb administers stitches. Richie McCaw drags himself out for the media. A few forwards shiver in large, ice-filled rubbish bins, a state-of-the-art recovery technique. Pacifica Rap plays, then some reggae.

After a while, Darren Shand, the manager, gently clears the room.

It is just the team. The inner sanctum. McCaw, Read, Thorn, Smith, Carter, Dagg, Muliaina. All household names. Squashed together on the benches, they look like huge schoolboys.

They debrief.

The session is chaired by Mils Muliaina. Injured, he is today's off-field captain. The etiquette is like a *whare*, a Māori meeting-house, where everyone is given the opportunity to speak, to say their truth, to tell their story.

Muliaina hands over to Steve Hansen, 'Shag', the assistant coach, whose assessment is direct and unsparing. It was good, he says, but not good enough. Plenty of work to do in the lineout.

Got to get that right. Other teams won't go so easy on us. Let's not get carried away. Let's not get ahead of ourselves. Some big games coming.

He hands on to Wayne Smith, the other assistant coach. Smithy is a taut, lean man with a shrewd, lined expression. He's a man who knows men, how they think, how they work, how to get the best from them; the guts of this team. He makes a few incisive points and hands on to 'Gilly', Nic Gill PhD, the conditioning coach, who hands on in turn to Graham Henry – 'Ted', the headmaster of the team, the head coach. A witty man, Henry's dry humour doesn't always carry on television. He is the boss here, the Svengali, the ringmaster for this roadshow.

> The challenge is to always improve, to always get better, even when you are the best. Especially when you are the best.

Henry congratulates McCaw on becoming the most successful captain in All Blacks history. Then he tells the team there's work to be done. A lot of work to be done.

Muliaina reminds the players to remember the sacrifices they have made to be in this room. Finally, he proposes a toast to McCaw.

'To Skip!' he says.

'To Skip,' the room replies.

'Well done, guys,' he says. 'Let's go.'

~

This is when something happens that you might not expect.

Two of the senior players – one an international player of the year, twice – each pick up a long-handled broom and begin to sweep the sheds. They brush the mud and the gauze into small piles in the corner.

While the country is still watching replays and schoolkids lie in bed dreaming of All Blacks' glory, the All Blacks themselves are tidying up after themselves.

Sweeping the sheds.

Doing it properly.

So no one else has to.

Because no one looks after the All Blacks.

The All Blacks look after themselves.

~

It's an 'example of personal discipline' says Andrew Mehrtens, former All Blacks fly-half (what New Zealanders call a first five eight) and the second highest All Blacks points scorer of all time.

'It's not expecting somebody else to do your job for you. It teaches you not to expect things to be handed to you.'

'If you have personal discipline in your life,' he says, 'then you are going to be more disciplined on the field. If you're wanting guys to pull together as a team, you've got to have that. You don't want a group of individuals.'

'It's not going to make you win all the time,' he says, 'but it's certainly going to make you better as a team over the long run.'

> A collection of talented individuals without personal discipline will ultimately and inevitably fail. Character triumphs over talent.

~

Vince Lombardi, the legendary coach of the Green Bay Packers American football team, inherited an outfit that was down on its luck. It had foundered at the bottom of the NFL for years and even the fans saw no way back. Lombardi took over the team in 1959. Two years later they won the NFL, and again in 1962 and 1965, followed by the Super Bowl in 1966 and 1967.

His success, he said, was based on what he called the 'Lombardi Model', which began with a simple statement:

_____ *Only by knowing yourself can you become an effective leader.*

For him, it all begins with self-knowledge, with the great 'I Am'; a fundamental understanding and appreciation of our own personal values. It was on this foundation that he built his teams and his success.

From self-knowledge, Lombardi believed, we develop character and integrity. And from character and integrity comes leadership.

Jon Kabat-Zinn (*In Wherever You Go, There You Are*) tells a story about Buckminster Fuller, the visionary architect and thinker.

Depressed and considering suicide, Fuller asked himself some questions that revolutionized his life:

_____ *'What is my job on the planet? What is it that needs doing, that I know something about, that probably won't happen unless I take responsibility for it?'*

These questions, in turn inspired Lombardi, and might in turn inspire us. This might mean taking responsibility for a team, for a company or for the lives of thousands; or it might be something as simple as sweeping the sheds. Either way, it begins with character, and character begins with humility. At the start of each season, Lombardi would hold up the pigskin and say, 'Gentlemen, this is a football.'

~

Under coach John Wooden, the UCLA Bruins basketball team won the US national collegiate championship for seven straight years, starting in 1967. At the start of each season, writer Claudia Luther reports, he would sit his team down in their locker room and, for a long time – for a very long time – they would learn how to put on their socks:

_____ *Check the heel area. We don't want any sign of a wrinkle about it . . . The wrinkle will be sure you get blisters, and those blisters are going to make you lose playing time, and if you're good enough, your loss of playing time might get the coach fired.*

The lesson wasn't really about blisters, or playing time, or whether the coach got fired. It was about doing the basics right, taking care of the details, looking after yourself and the team. It was about humility.

'Winning takes talent,' John Wooden would say. 'To repeat it takes character.'

Like the All Blacks head coach Graham Henry, John Wooden was a teacher. Which is no coincidence.

~

Another remarkable man was American football coach Bill Walsh, who also considered himself a teacher first, a leader second.

Between 1979 and 1989, Walsh coached the San Francisco 49ers from an underperforming bunch of also-rans into one of the great sporting dynasties in gridiron history by employing a similar philosophy. He believed that, 'You get nowhere without character. Character is essential to individuals, and their cumulative character is the backbone of your winning team.'

Create the highest possible operating standards, develop the character of your players, develop the culture of your team and, as the title of Walsh's book proclaims, *The Score Takes Care of Itself.*

'Walsh knew,' Stuart Lancaster, the current England rugby coach, told rugby writer Mark Reason, 'that if you established a culture higher than that of your opposition, you would win. So rather than obsessing about the results, you focus on the team.'

'The challenge of every team is to build a feeling of oneness, of dependence on one another,' said Vince Lombardi. 'Because the question is usually not how well each person performs, but how well they work together.'

> Collective character is vital to success. Focus on getting the culture right; the results will follow.

Owen Eastwood is a man of many talents. A lawyer for clients including the All Blacks, he has also worked as a consultant for the South African Proteas, NATO Command and other organizations on culture creation programs. Eastwood uses the equation:

$$Performance = Capability + Behaviour$$

The way you behave, he argues, will either bring out the best or worst of your capability, and this applies to businesses and teams as well as to individuals. 'Leaders create the right environment for the right behaviours to occur,' says Eastwood. 'That's their primary role.'

Behaviour exists in two domains, he continues: Public and Private.

'The Public Domain' means those areas of a player's life when he is under team protocol – whether at training, during a game, travelling or on promotional duty. Professionalism, physical application and proficiency are demanded here.

'The Private Domain' is the one in which we spend time with ourselves and where our mind-game plays out. This is the biggest game of all, as daily we confront our habits, limitations, temptations and fears.

'Leaders design and create an environment,' says Eastwood, 'which drives the high performance behaviours needed for success. The really clever teams build a culture that drives the behaviours they need.'

'I think all of those environments,' says Graham Henry, 'whether it's a business environment or sporting environment, are about developing people. So, if you develop your people, your business is going to be more successful. It's just a matter of creating an environment where that becomes a happening every day.'

Every day? In organizations all around the world, leaders sally forth with inspiring messages of change. Everyone congratulates them on a presentation well delivered, admires the slogan, tucks the brand book into their briefcase, and then goes back to their desks and does nothing.

Alternatively, the leaders feverishly develop and distribute an action plan, calibrated to the finest detail, with no real understanding of the vision, purpose or principles behind it.

This is how Will Hogg describes what he calls the 'Vision into Action' paradox. Hogg, who runs Kinetic, a Geneva-based management consultancy that works with the leaders of large organizations to deliver culture change and engagement, likes to use the Japanese proverb:

_____ *Vision without action is a dream.*

Action without vision is a nightmare.

'The paradox,' he says, 'is that, though every organization thinks they have unique problems, many change issues are centred on one thing. The ability – or inability – to convert vision into action. Sometimes it is through a lack of a vision itself. More often through the inability to translate vision into simple, ordinary, everyday actions.'

Actions like senior leaders who sweep the floor.

~

'Talent was irrelevant,' says Wayne Smith. He is not talking about the All Blacks now, but the Chiefs, the team he went on to after leaving the All Blacks fold, but the principles are the same. 'We carefully picked the players. We used matrices to back intuition, because there are certain stats in rugby that determine the player's character and that's what we were after. So we picked high work rate, strong body movers, guys that were unselfish and had a sacrificial mindset.'

They selected on character.

~

Ethos is the Greek word for character. Descended from the same root as the word ethics, it is used to describe the beliefs, principles, values, codes and culture of an organization. It is the 'way we do things around here', the unwritten (and sometimes written) rules, the moral character of a particular group of people. It is the place we live, our certitude and rectitude, our base.

> Our values decide our character.
> Our character decides our value.

Values provide the bedrock of belief. Any lasting organization – from churches to states, companies to causes – has enshrined at their heart a fundamental set of principles: 'Faith, Hope and Charity'; 'Liberté, égalité, fraternité'.

A values-based, purpose-driven culture is a foundation of the All Blacks' approach and sustained success. But, as any business leader knows, value-words like integrity, sacrifice, determination, imagination, innovation, collaboration, persistence, responsibility, and so on, seem powerful in the abstract, but can be flat and generic on the page. The challenge is always to bring them to life, and into the lives of those you lead. As we shall see, the All Blacks are a world class case study in how to do this. Their management are past-masters at turning vision into everyday action, purpose into practice.

In fact, in answer to the question, 'What is the All Blacks' competitive advantage?', key is the ability to manage their culture and central narrative by attaching the players' personal meaning to a higher purpose. It is the identity of the team that matters – not so much what the All Blacks do, but who they are, what they stand for, and why they exist.

After all, the All Blacks' competitive advantage does not come from player numbers: England have more rugby players than the rest of the world combined. Despite the misconception in the UK's popular press, it's also not about race: the first Polynesian to play for the All Blacks, Bryan Williams, only did so in 1970 and the All Blacks had already led the world for most of that century. Diversity helps, yes, but it's not the whole story.

> 'What is my job on the planet? What is it that needs doing, that I know something about, that probably won't happen unless I take responsibility for it?'
>
> Buckminster Fuller

It's not just infrastructure – the 'rugby stairway' – though this technical framework, combined with the relentless desire to 'be an All Black', certainly helps propel talent through the lower grades and on towards sporting immortality.

The All Blacks' remarkable success on the field begins with a very particular culture off the field and it is this culture – the glue that holds it all together – that has delivered extrordinary competitive advantage for more than a century.

To become an All Black means becoming a steward of a cultural legacy. Your role is to *leave the jersey in a better place*. The humility, expectation and responsibility that this brings lifts their game. It makes them the best in the world.

What this means for leaders in other fields is the story of this book.

~

The revitalization of the All Blacks culture between 2004 and 2011 began with some fundamental questions: What is the meaning of being an All Black? What does it mean to be a New Zealander? These questions, and an ongoing interrogative process, were central in the re-establishment of a values-driven, purpose-driven culture.

This management technique – which begins with questions – is of the 'Socratic Method', so called because Socrates used a type of interrogation to separate his pupils from their prejudices. The goal? To help them find self-knowledge, even if the truth turns out to be uncomfortable.

It is a key technique within the All Blacks leadership and captured in a Māori proverb:

_____ *Waiho kia pātai ana, he kaha ui te kaha.*
Let the questioning continue; the ability of the person is in asking questions.

Rather than just instruct outwards, the coaches began to ask questions; first of themselves – how can we do this better? – and then of their players – what do you think? This interrogative culture, in which the individual makes their own judgements, and sets their own internal benchmarks, became increasingly important.

A culture of asking and re-asking fundamental questions cuts away unhelpful beliefs in order to achieve clarity of execution. Humility allows us to ask a simple question: how can we do this better?

The questions the leaders asked of themselves, and of the team, was the beginning of a rugby revolution.

~

The word decide comes from 'to cut away'. The All Blacks' interrogative culture cuts away unhelpful beliefs in order to achieve clarity.

It is a facilitated style of interpersonal leadership in a learning environment concerned with adaptive problem solving and continuous improvement and in which humility – not knowing all the answers – delivers strength.

'You can guide,' says Wayne Smith, 'but I'm a great believer in that we don't instruct a lot. If you believe that attitude you've got to ask questions – and we try and get descriptive answers so you get self-awareness.'

_____ *'What might happen if...?'*
'In this situation what would you do...?'
'How might you...?'
'What about...?'

This questioning is as applicable to business as it is to rugby. No one person has all the answers, but asking questions challenges the status quo, helps connect with core values and beliefs, and is a catalyst for individual improvement.

After all, the better the questions we ask, the better the answers we get.

~

Clearly the All Blacks are an exceptional environment. Their elite status, constant scrutiny and the resources at their disposal set them apart from, say, a sales team in Wolverhampton or a marketing business in Duluth. There are different pressures, different rewards, different measures. However, it is possible to extract some useful lessons from this, the world's most successful team, based on simple shared humanity and the application of common sense. So, although a study of what makes the All Blacks tick might not have all the answers, it does enable us to begin to address some important questions of leadership.

~

The Māori carvings with which tourists to New Zealand soon become familiar are called *whakairo*. These represent the tribal *tīpuna*, the Ancestors, and have been carved in commemoration of their deeds. They tell stories of love and death and great bravery. Though they are a gallery of heroes there is no vanity in their depiction – deliberately grotesque, their tongues protrude, their features are distorted.

Humility is deeply ingrained in Māori and broader Polynesian culture and, indeed, the word Māori implies 'normal' or 'natural' to distinguish the people of the land from the gods above. To 'get above yourself' is deeply frowned upon in this culture, and more broadly in New Zealand society.

It should be our acts that remain after us, the *whakairo* remind us, not our vainglory. Humility is seen as a vital part of a well-adjusted character. It is essential to *mana*, the Māori and Polynesian word that captures so many qualities; authority, status, personal power, bearing, charisma and, according to *The New Zealand Dictionary*, 'great personal prestige and character'.

> Humility does not mean weakness, but its opposite. Leaders with *mana* understand the strength of humility. It allows them to connect with their deepest values and the wider world.

For Māori, and within the All Blacks, *mana* is perhaps the ultimate accolade, the underlying spiritual goal of human existence. Linguists have recognized the relationship between the word and the 'powerful forces of nature such as thunder and storm winds that were conceived as the expression of an unseen supernatural agency' *(Coddington)*. Others have argued that it is the universal life force that is the very origin of our ideas of God. Certainly, it describes a person of rare quality; a natural leader possessing strength, leadership, great personal power, gentleness – and humility.

When asked about Chris Ashton, the English winger, and his habit of swan-diving for a try, former All Blacks captain and hooker Anton Oliver says, 'We'd just die.'

For leaders of all stripes, reconnecting with our values – with our truest, deepest instincts – is an essential building block of character, which is the essence of leadership. And it begins with humility. St Augustine said it best: 'Lay first the foundation of humility ... The higher your structure is to be, the deeper must be its foundation.'

So, as these sporting superstars clean up their locker room, looking after themselves so that no one else has to, we might ask ourselves if excellence – true excellence – begins with humility; with a humble willingness to 'sweep the sheds'.

After all, what else is a legacy if not that which you leave behind after you have gone?

Sweep the Sheds

The great sports coaches of the past such as John Wooden and Vince Lombardi put humility at the core of their teaching. The All Blacks place a similar emphasis on their fundamental and foundational values, going so far as to select on character over talent. The players are taught never to get too big to do the small things that need to be done. 'Exceptional results demand exceptional circumstances,' says Wayne Smith. These conditions help shape the culture and therefore the ethos – the character – of the team. Humility begins at the level of interpersonal communication, enabling an interrogative, highly facilitated learning environment in which no one has all the answers. Each individual is invited to contribute solutions to the challenges being posed. This is a key component of building sustainable competitive advantage through cultural cohesion. It leads to innovation, increased self knowledge, and greater character. It leads towards *mana*.

Sweep the Sheds

Never be too big to do the small things that need to be done.

_____ *Kāore te kūmara e whāki ana tana reka.*

The kūmara (sweet potato) does not need to say how sweet he is.

II

ADAPT

_____ *Māui – the discoverer of the secret of fire – was spearing birds with his brothers one day. But as his spear had no barbs, their prey escaped them. Māui's mother told him to use sticks to create barbs for his weapon – which he did. They feasted on kererū (pigeon) that night.*

GO FOR THE GAP
When you're on top of
your game, change
your game

Somewhere over the Indian Ocean, on a long, disconsolate flight between South Africa and New Zealand, the new All Blacks assistant coach, Wayne Smith, turned to Darren Shand, his team manager, and told him, 'We have a dysfunctional team – if it's not fixed, I won't be back.'

The All Blacks had just lost to South Africa 40-26, finishing last in the annual Tri-Nations tournament. For a team attuned to winning, and with the highest 'kill rate' in world sport, it was a disaster. But, as Bob Howitt tells it in *Final Word*, worse was to follow that night at the team hotel.

A 'Court Session', a mock trial fuelled by the forced consumption of alcohol, had left some very famous faces chronically drunk; some so much so that they were worried for their lives. It was later reported that some of the Springbok players, billeted in the same hotel and returning from a meal to celebrate their series victory, had to extract various All Blacks from hallways, bushes and gutters and put them in the recovery position.

Something had to change.

'The way we were going was not going to cut the mustard in the professional era,' says Gilbert Enoka, the tall, personable mental skills coach. 'You can't work all week and then have Saturday night through to Monday off where you bloody drink and sink.'

Graham Henry, the head coach, had only recently been entrusted with the top job in New Zealand sport. After the debacle, Smith slipped him a note insisting that we 'fix this thing.'

It was the beginning of a long, painstaking and often painful process that eventually led to Rugby World Cup glory. What these men – Henry, Smith, Hansen, Enoka, Shand, together with the players – achieved is a case study in transformational culture change, its lessons applicable well beyond the rugby field.

~

Will Hogg believes that effective organizational change requires four key stages. The absence of any one factor, the management consultant says, will inhibit culture change and often make it impossible:

> **Four Stages for Organizational Change:**
> ° A Case for Change;
> ° A Compelling Picture of the Future;
> ° A Sustained Capability to Change;
> ° A Credible Plan to Execute.

The **Case for Change** for the All Blacks was clear. Performance was sub-par, both on and off the field. 'I wasn't in the room,' says former All Blacks captain, Anton Oliver, 'but it started by Tana [Umaga, the then captain] saying, "I don't really want to play, I'm scared of playing. I'm not enjoying it." Everyone had been locked in their own little islands feeling the same thing.' They had lost, to use Gilbert Enoka's phrase, 'the being of team'. There was a strong case for change.

Next, the team required a **Compelling Picture of the Future**. In the next chapter we look at the role of purpose and personal meaning, and how a three-day crisis meeting set the framework that would culminate in Rugby World Cup victory. First, though, there needed to be a clear strategy for change. This was articulated by Graham Henry (as reported in *Final Word* and repeated in interviews) as the creation of 'an environment . . . that would stimulate the players and make them want to take part in it'. Henry realized that the world was changing and the All Blacks, like any other business – 'and it is a business' – were competing on the open market for the best human resources. He reasoned that an active focus on personal development and leadership would create capacity, capability and loyalty.

Third, the team required the right **Sustained Capability to Change**. This meant eliminating players who were seen as hindering the chance for change and, more importantly, building the capability of those who remained and those who joined. This centred on a 'dual-management' model in which responsibility was 'handed over' to the players so that they had, in Henry's phrase, 'more skin in the game'.

> A winning organization is an environment of personal and professional development, in which each individual takes responsibility and shares ownership.

It also involved – and this is where Henry the educator excelled – the creation of a learning environment, which acted as a stepladder of personal and professional development. The creation of a 'Leadership Group' as well as 'Individual Operating Units' in which players took increasing responsibility for team protocols, principles and culture, gave structure to this strategy. Captain Richie McCaw believes it to be the most important innovation of Henry's reign.

Leaders create leaders.

Fourth, the team required a **Credible Plan to Execute**. In this the leadership, with their unique shared structure, excelled. Steered by Henry, the men were able to develop and deploy a self-reflective, self-adjusting plan that developed the technical, tactical, physical, logistical and psychological capabilities of their collective.

The plan traversed years, seasons, series, weeks, days and even the seconds the match clock travelled as it counted down to the final whistle. It was a plan executed in public on the field of play, but calibrated behind the scenes, and which led to the most successful period of All Blacks rugby in history.

And a small gold cup.

~

We shouldn't be too surprised that the All Blacks culture had begun to rot from the inside. Unless intervention occurs, all organizational cultures do. The Court Sessions, a hangover from the days of amateurism and a by-product of New Zealand's wider binge drinking culture, were merely a symptom of a more general and inevitable process, described in graphic form by the Sigmoid Curve.

Though it is tempting to see life, business, society and success as part of a linear progression of constant and never-ending refinement and growth, the opposite is true. Like most things in nature, cultures are subject to a more *cyclical* process, of ebb and flow, growth and decline. According to Charles Handy (in *The Empty Raincoat*), this cycle has three distinct phases: Learning, Growth and Decline.

In the **Learning Phase**, we often experience dips in actual performance as we feel our way through the unfamiliar. Think of Tiger Woods relearning his golf swing or the teething period in which a new CEO gets to grips with the issues of an organization.

Then once the learning has become embedded and momentum builds, so growth accelerates. This is the **Growth Phase**. Rewards follow. Praise and blandishments too. Soon we're on top of the game and on top of the world. We're invincible, our success assured. And so begins the Fall.

The **Decline Phase** hits us much like the early twinges of arthritis in a middle-aged person. At first an anomaly, it eventually becomes the painful norm. Soon we're staring at the hollowed-out cheeks of an old person in the mirror, wondering whatever happened to our gilded youth.

The key, of course, is when we're on top of our game, to change our game; to exit relationships, recruit new talent, alter tactics, reassess strategy. To make what Handy describes as 'Sigmoid leaps', a series of scalloped jumps along the Sigmoid Curve, outwitting inevitability.

As a leader this is one of our primary responsibilities, and the skill comes in timing these leaps: when to axe your star performer; when to blood new talent; when to change your game-plan altogether. As the *Encyclopedia of Leadership* asks:

_____ *What steps do you need to consider taking so you can prepare for the second curve, without prematurely leaving your current success (on the first curve) behind?*

This is the quintessence of *kaizen*, the Japanese notion of continuous improvement. 'The idea,' writes Bunji Tozawa, in a professional white paper, 'is to nurture the company's human resources.' Originally, *kaizen* was less a productivity enhancer than a 'culture creator', a way in which Japanese business could engage and inspire their workforce – to, in Graham Henry's strategic statement, 'stimulate the players and make them want to take part in it'.

> Organizational decline is inevitable unless leaders prepare for change – even when standing at the pinnacle of success.

~

25

The military have an acronym: VUCA: Volatile, Uncertain, Complex and Ambiguous. VUCA describes a world prone to sudden change, unknown consequence and complex, shifting interrelationships; one that is difficult to decipher, impossible to predict. For the military-industrial complex, VUCA means asymmetric warfare, geopolitical instability and unreliable loyalties. For business, it means structural collapse, credit crises, reputation damage. For individuals, it represents career insecurity, rising prices, housing market illiquidity and an uncertain future. For leaders, it means dealing with decisions that involve incomplete knowledge, sketchy resources and the vicissitudes of human nature.

In his seminal paper 'Destruction and Creation', the military strategist John R. Boyd created a theory with direct applicability to a fast-changing environment. 'To maintain an accurate or effective grasp of reality,' he argued, 'one must undergo a continuous cycle of interaction with the environment to assess its constant changes.' He asked himself, 'how do we create the mental concepts to support decision making activity?'

His answer was the Decision Cycle or OODA Loop.

OODA stands for Observe, Orient, Decide and Act. It is quick to apply, and useful for everyday decision-making.

Observe

This is data collection through the senses; visual, auditory, tactile, olfactory, taste – as well as more modern metrics. Like an animal sniffing the wind, we gather the raw material for response.

Orient

This is analysis, synthesizing all available data into a single, coherent 'map of the territory' – a working theory of our options.

Decide

This is the point of choice; where we determine the best course of action. We cut away the extraneous by making a decision.

Act

We execute; acting swiftly and decisively to take advantage of the moment. We then go back to the beginning and observe the effect of our actions. And so the loop continues.

Boyd's analysis of dogfights over Korea had shown that the pilots who got inside the OODA loop first were those who survived. To prevail in conflict, Boyd says, we 'must be able to form mental concepts of observed reality, as we perceive it, and be able to change these concepts as reality itself begins to change'.

Boyd's theories are remarkably similar to those of Alexander Vasilyevich Suvorov, a Russian general born in 1719 who wrote the military manual *The Science of Victory*. He believed in:

> 'It is not the strongest species that survive, nor the most intelligent, but the ones most responsive to change.'
>
> Charles Darwin

Hystrota	playing a fast-paced game
Glazometer	making quick decisions that disorient the opposition
Natisk	acting aggressively to seize the competitive advantage

That is, move rapidly into a commanding position, assess your unfolding options quickly and clearly, attack with absolute and ruthless commitment – assess, adjust and repeat.

Or as the All Blacks would put it:

_____ *Go for the gap.*

For Boyd, Suvorov and the All Blacks, adaptation is not a reaction, but a systematic series of actions. It isn't just reacting to what's happening in the moment, it is being the agent of change. This is achieved through a structured feedback loop – by building the adaptive process into the very way we lead.

How does this work in practice? Kevin Roberts, CEO of Saatchi & Saatchi, talks about 100-day plans:

_____ *Getting started is deceptively simple. First list around 10 things you need to achieve over the next 100 days. Start each plan with an Action Verb and use no more than 3 words each. Make sure each action is measurable and that each one is a stretch. You'll know when something is a real stretch and when you're just creating a list with things you can tick off. Review your list every Friday morning. When the 100 Days comes round, the goal is to have each item checked off. All you need to do then is get a sheet of A4 paper and get started.*

Whereas once 50 per cent of his time was spent on assessment, he explains, and 20 per cent on execution, today all information is instantaneous. Consequently 70 per cent of his time – and that of the company's other leaders – is now spent on execution.

A committed All Blacks fan, Roberts, who was born in Britain and made his home in New Zealand, was instrumental as head of Saatchi & Saatchi Wellington in developing the All Blacks' brand in the professional era. When asked what he's learned from the All Blacks and how they inspire him, he answers:

'It's about going for the gap.'

It's about adapting quickly to change by creating an adaptive culture.

~

In 2004, the All Blacks faced a precipice.

With results declining, key players threatening to leave and cultural dysfunction endemic, the management had to act and act quickly. In his report to New Zealand Rugby Union at the end of that year (as recounted in Bob Howitt's *Final Word*), Graham Henry identified his key areas of focus:

○ Sufficient leadership, knowledge and confidence to implement the game plan
○ The transference of leadership and therefore responsibility from the coaches to the players
○ The development of leadership ability and composure
○ The necessity for the group to understand their identity – who they are, what they stand for, and their collective and individual responsibilities as All Blacks

The following chapters outline the actions the leadership took to turn their vision into action – and the 15 key lessons we can learn and apply to our own particular field of play.

So that we too can go for the gap.

Go for the Gap

Momentum swings faster than we think. One moment we're on top of the world, the next falling off the other side. The role of the leader is to know when to reinvent, and how to do it.

The Sigmoid Curve means that when we're at the top of the game, it's time to change our game. The key is not losing momentum. As the military have discovered, the best form of attack is a continuous feedback loop and, as we know from *kaizen*, this process is best when it involves your people. The teams that will thrive in this VUCA world are those who act quickly and decisively to seize competitive advantage; adjusting and readjusting along the way. You either adapt, or you lose; and sustainable competitive advantage is achieved by the development of a continuously self-adjusting culture. Adaption is not a reaction, but continual action, so plan to respond.

Go for the Gap

When you're on top of your game, change your game.

_____ *I orea te tuatara, ka puta ki waho.*

When poked at with a stick, the tuatara will emerge.

(A problem is solved by continuing to find solutions.)

III

PURPOSE

—— *He rangi tā Matawhāiti,*
he rangi tā Matawhānui.
The person with a narrow vision sees a narrow horizon,
the person with a wide vision sees a wide horizon.

PLAY WITH PURPOSE
Ask 'Why?'

New Zealand Rugby Union Headquarters, Wellington, 2004

Soon after that long, painful flight back from South Africa landed, eight men found a small meeting room in the headquarters of the NZRU and sat down to 'fix this thing'.

In the room were Henry, his assistants Smith and Hansen, Enoka, the mental skills coach, Darren Shand, the team manager, Brian Lochore, former captain, coach and team manager, All Blacks captain Tana Umaga and his then vice-captain, Richie McCaw. The meeting was to last three days.

Graham Henry describes it as the most important conversation of his All Blacks' career. It would result in the complete overhaul of the most successful sporting culture in human history.

The key insight came from the old warhorse, Brian Lochore. Pondering the strategic objective – to create 'an environment ... that would stimulate the players and make them want to take part in it' – he came up with the six words that would define the efforts of the next eight or so years:

_____ *Better People Make Better All Blacks*

That is, by developing the individual players and giving them the tools, skills and character that they needed to contribute beyond the rugby field, they would also, in theory, develop the tools, skills and character to contribute more effectively on it.

This 'Kiwi *kaizen*' was a focus on personal development, both as human beings and as professional sportsmen, so that they had the character, composure, and people skills to be leaders, both on and off the field.

The challenge was to make this work in practice. 'There

was no blueprint,' says Graham Henry. 'You couldn't just look it up on the internet.'

How they managed it – and turned their vision into action – provides invaluable insight for business leaders looking to effect culture change that delivers sustainable competitive advantage.

~

In many ways, the story begins back in 1997 in the pretty, provincial city of Christchurch, nestled in earthquake country on the edge of the Canterbury Plains. This Cathedral City is the crucible

Better People Make Better Leaders

of New Zealand rugby, and the heart of this particular All Blacks team. Most of the men in that three-day meeting in Wellington in 2004 had a strong connection to the Canterbury Crusaders, including Henry, Smith and McCaw, the current Crusaders captain.

Back in 1997, right at the beginning of professionalism, the Crusaders were just starting out; and it hadn't started well. As Wayne Smith says, the problem was that 'There wasn't an existing culture.'

The new 'franchise' had yet to win the hearts of the locals. It was made up of players from all over the country, diluting any local allegiance, and was suffering an identity crisis.

'We all bought into an idea of trying to create our own culture,' says Smith, 'and to do that we used storytelling. We had to put forward stuff that inspired us and that inspired the players.' He says, 'I really wanted the campaign to be vision driven and values based.'

He adds, 'If you are going to set goals [the players have] got to set goals. If you're going to be vision-driven and values-based, they have got to be a huge part of setting that.'

Smith says, 'Whether it's family, whether it's legacy, whether it's enhancing the jersey, whatever, you need to identify what it is [that gives the players purpose] so that you remain driven.' He adds, 'It's about purpose and personal meaning . . . Those are the two big things.'

'The more you have to play for,' Gilbert Enoka summarizes, 'the better you play.'

To turn their vision into something that the players could identify with, they needed a theme. The first came from Shakespeare's *Henry V*: 'for he today who sheds his blood with me shall be my brother'.

'We wanted to establish what a Crusader man would look like, what would drive him,' says Smith. 'It took a couple of weeks really to make sure that everyone bought into what we came up with, what the players came up with.'

The Crusaders had lost their first season of Super Rugby. After Smith and Enoka's intervention during 1997, they won the competition in 1998 and another six times over the next decade. They are the most successful outfit in Super Rugby history.

They became, in Enoka's phrase, 'the being of team.'

~

'The emotional glue of any culture – religion, nation or team – is its sense of identity and purpose,' says Owen Eastwood. What we identify with are the 'things we recognize as important to ourselves – to our deepest values . . . this kind of meaning has the emotional power to shape behaviour'.

This connection of personal meaning to public purpose is something the All Blacks focus on, almost obsessively: 'It's about

> Leaders connect personal meaning to a higher purpose to create belief and a sense of direction.

what you bring today,' says Enoka, 'and how you're going to fill that jersey.'

Personal meaning is the way we connect to a wider team purpose. If our values and beliefs are aligned with the values and beliefs of the organization, then we will work harder towards its success. If not, our individual motivation and purpose will suffer, and so will the organization.

Good leaders understand this and work hard to create a sense of connection, collaboration and communion. 'Purpose relates to an overarching goal beyond the practical missions that are pursued day in day out,' writes Eastwood. 'This drives the individual's intrinsic motivation, and gives a reason to belong, and a reason to sacrifice.'

The subject of 'identity' is so big in organizational culture, of course, that brand consultancies, advertising agencies and engagement specialists all vie for the opportunity to define and deliver it. In this space, business strategy, vision, values and purpose conjoin with corporate identity, design, advertising and communications to deliver powerful shifts of mindset and behaviours within teams and organizations.

It begins from the inside out.

As *New York Times* columnist Daniel Pink explains in his book *Drive*, 'Humans, by their nature, seek purpose – a cause greater and more enduring than themselves.' The most convincing arguments for his theories are the simplest to understand:

'We leave well paying jobs for purpose-driven ones.'

'We volunteer.'

'We have children!'

Pink argues that 'purpose maximization' is taking its place alongside profit maximization as an aspiration and a guiding principle for businesses around the world. His work reflects the 'Hawthorne Effect', the idea that emotional reward is more important than material compensation. That intrinsic rather than extrinsic motivation rules the world.

This aligns with Abraham Maslow and his famous 'Hierarchy of Needs'. Maslow thought that, once beyond the satisfaction and security of your basic needs – safety, food, water, shelter, warmth, comfort – you are no longer driven by purely extrinsic motivations and can turn your attention to deeper needs. The first, a sense of belonging and love; a partner, a family. From then on, life becomes about esteem; self respect, the respect of others, recognition for our talent, our capabilities, our behaviours.

In Maslow's world, we all move towards a sense of self-actualization. That is, a psychological state of presence, flow, self-respect, self-expression and authenticity.

This also aligns with the work of psychotherapist Victor Frankl, who, in *Man's Search for Meaning*, cites research from Johns Hopkins University:

_____ *Asked what they considered 'very important' to them now, 16% checked 'making a lot of money'; 78% said their first goal was 'finding a meaning and purpose to my life.'*

'What man actually needs,' argues Frankl, 'is not a tension-less state but rather the striving and struggling for a worthwhile goal, a freely chosen task.'

'Being human always points, and is directed, to something, or someone, other than oneself,' he writes. 'The more one forgets himself – by giving himself to a cause to serve or another person to love – the more human he is, and the more he actualizes himself.'

'Self-actualization,' he concludes, 'is possible only as a side-effect of self-transcendence.'

Of 'getting over yourself'.

Of sweeping the sheds.

And it begins with the question 'Why?'

~

According to Walter Isaacson in his book, *Steve Jobs*, the Apple founder once told his team: 'the work fifty people are doing here is going to send a ripple right through the universe.' He later said, 'The goal was never to beat the competition or to make a lot of money. It was to do the greatest thing possible, or even a little greater.' It was the purpose, the passion and the products that mattered and made ripples – while the profits followed in great waves. 'You should never start a company with the goal of getting rich,' Mike Markkula, Apple's 'Employee Number 3', had told Jobs. 'Your goal should be making something you believe in and making a company that will last.'

In another example, Howard Schultz of Starbucks began his company with a singular, some might say altruistic, purpose: to create a company where health cover for employees was standard. Fuelled by memories of his father struggling through a succession of low-paid jobs with no health care, this was his purpose above and beyond selling coffee. He sees this as the fundamental cause of his success. 'People want to be part of something larger than themselves. They want to be part of something they're really proud of, that they'll fight for, sacrifice for, that they trust.'

Saatchi & Saatchi wants 'to make the world a better place for everyone'. Ford wants to 'democratize the automobile'. Disney brings 'smiles to the faces of children'. Nike 'empowers the individual'. P&G are on a 'relentless quest to be the best', while for Toyota, 'there is always a better way'.

Barcelona FC, meanwhile, is driven by perhaps the most motivating purpose of them all: they play for Catalonia; they 'play for freedom'.

Jim Collins, in *Good to Great*, describes this as the 'extra dimension' – a guiding philosophy that consists of core values and a core purpose beyond just making money. He believes that, when authentic and rigorously adhered to, a dramatic, compelling purpose is a fundamental driver of the companies that go from good to great.

'Reason leads to conclusions,' Canadian neurologist Donald Calne says, 'Emotion leads to action.' If you want higher performance, begin with a higher purpose.

Begin by asking, 'Why?'

~

As well as Graham Henry, there is another TED, the famous series of annual seminars and video presentations described on its internet site as 'Ideas Worth Sharing'.

One of the most watched videos on the TED site is a presentation by Simon Sinek, author of *Start With Why*, who expresses what most of us innately know: 'people don't buy what you do, they buy *why* you do it'. He argues that, because of the limbic – a nerve centre buried deep within the pre-linguistic core of our brain – the way we feel about something is more important than what we think about it. That, when given a choice, we follow our gut.

Sinek told an audience at the United States Air Force Weapons School, 'What I'm interested in is what gets people up every single day to do something, maybe pay a premium, maybe suffer inconvenience, maybe sacrifice because they're driven by something else. What is that thing? What I've learned is it's that question, why. It has a biological imperative, it drives us, it inspires us.'

He argues that inspired leaders and organizations, regardless of their size and industry, all think, act and communicate from the 'inside out.' After all, he says in his TED speech, Martin Luther King 'gave the "I have a dream" speech, not the "I have a plan" speech . . . If you hire people who believe what you believe, they'll work for you with blood, sweat and tears.'

> Inspired leaders, organizations and teams find their deepest purpose – their 'why?' – and attract followers through shared values, vision and beliefs.

As Nietzsche said: 'He who has a *why* to live for can bear almost any *how*.'

It's at the core of the vision and value-based mindset.

~

When Owen Eastwood began working with the Proteas, the South African cricket team, the side was languishing at number four in the world rankings. Psychologically they had 'lost their way'. In a collaborative process, involving players, coaches, management and even a cross-section of the non-playing public, Eastwood helped the team 'rediscover' a word from the Bantu languages, *Ubuntu*. It has now become the central organizing thought for the team – its reason for being.

Its reason why.

Ubuntu is 'the essence of being human,' says Bishop Desmond Tutu. '*Ubuntu* speaks particularly about the fact that you can't exist as a human being in isolation. It speaks about our interconnectedness.' *Ubuntu* does not mean that people should not have self-interest, said Nelson Mandela in interview with journalist Tim Modesi. But 'are you going to do so in order to enable the community around you to be able to improve? These are the important things in life.'

Ubuntu means we send out ripples from us into the wider community: our actions affect everyone, not just us. The Proteas embrace this ripple effect and the inspiration they have on the whole of South Africa. And it lifts them.

They play for something greater than themselves.

~

Meanwhile, years after Smith and Enoka moved on, the Crusaders' vision is still tangibly expressed in their strategy room. In *The Real McCaw*, author Greg McGee describes how one wall is dominated by a grey polystyrene archway of Corinthian columns, plinths, gables and foundation stones. It looks like a Walt Disney version of a Greek temple. At the base are foundation stones with words written on them. 'Team-First' is at the centre, surrounded by the Crusader's other funda-mental values: 'Loyalty', 'Integrity', 'Respect', 'Work-Ethic' and 'Enjoyment'. Across the central plinth is one word, 'Excellence', the ultimate aim.

Connecting the foundation with the apex is a series of columns, each of which has a title: 'Nutrition', 'Physical', 'Technical', 'Practical', 'Teamness' and 'Mental'. It is these six pillars upon which excellence – and success – is built.

'It's funny how often, if the team's not going well,' McCaw says, 'you look at those foundation stones and find the reason in there somewhere.'

~

It's easy to be cynical but there is little doubt this stuff works. Just as the Crusaders under Smith went on to dominate Super Rugby, the Proteas found success through the self-discovery of a common purpose. On 28 August 2012, with 'Ubuntu' as their mantra, they became the first team to be world number one in all three formats of the game.

Similarly, Graham Henry's All Blacks, after their inauspicious start, and by consistent application of storytelling techniques, a devolved leadership strategy, the creation of a learning environment and a focus on the mind game, completed his reign with a winning record of 86 per cent – and a Rugby World Cup.

~

So, if the key strategic driver was 'Better People Make Better All Blacks', what is their fundamental purpose? What is the 'why?'

Officially, according to the NZRU literature, it is to 'unite and inspire New Zealand'. But it goes deeper than that. 'We're lucky in that we have a huge history which is motivational to the current team,' says Graham Henry. 'It's hugely important to the current guys who carry the responsibility – because their job is to add to the legacy.'

To add to the legacy.

'There's a rich tradition of players who have had that stewardship,' says Wayne Smith, 'to enhance the jersey and pass it on in a better state than what it was when you got it.' As former All Black Ali Williams puts it, 'you have to leave the jersey in a better place'.

'All I was doing,' says legendary former All Blacks captain Sean Fitzpatrick, 'was trying to make it a better team to pass on to the next generation. And in saying that,' he continues, 'the underlying word would be winning. We have to continue that legacy.'

They have to play a bigger game.

~

Back in the small room in Wellington in 2004, the heroes of this story were still a long way from leaving either the jersey or the statistics in a better place.

According to Graham Henry, it wasn't until the All Blacks played France in Paris at the end of that year's European tour that the first glimmers of hope began to show.

On that day, the All Blacks scored five tries to none, demolishing the French 45-6. For the first time, this group of All Blacks showed what they were capable of achieving; what was inside them.

Upon his return from Europe, Bob Howitt records in *Final Word*, Henry wrote his report to the NZRU:

> _____ *Contributing to the success was the implementation of a leadership group . . . The players gained a great understanding and respect for each other as they developed. They grew to understand they had similar challenges as international rugby players and these challenges were better handled collectively than individually. This brought togetherness – they were 'one'. They . . . went to 'war' for each other.*

'My army won because they knew what they were fighting for,' said Oliver Cromwell, 'and loved what they knew.' For a warrior tribe from New Zealand, it was the beginning of the being of team.

––––––––––––

Play with Purpose

Our fundamental human drive comes from within – from intrinsic rather than extrinsic motivations. Leaders who harness the power of purpose have the ability to galvanize a group, aligning its behaviours to the strategic pillars of the enterprise.

Using vivid storytelling techniques, including themes, symbols, imagery, rituals, mantras and metaphor, and bringing them to life with imagination and flair, leaders create a sense of inclusion, connectedness and unity – a truly collective, collaborative mindset. It begins by asking 'Why? Why are we doing this? Why am I sacrificing myself for this project? What is the higher purpose?' The answers to these questions have the ability to transform the fortunes of a group or enterprise – activating individuals, providing a cultural glue, guiding behaviours and creating an overall sense of purpose and personal connection. It is the beginning of the being of team.

Play with Purpose
Ask 'Why?'

Whāia e koe ki te iti kahurangi;
ki te tuohu koe, me he maunga teitei.
Seek the treasure you value most dearly;
if you bow your head, let it be to a lofty mountain.

IV

RESPONSIBILITY

—— *Haere taka mua, taka muri; kaua e whai.*
Be a leader, not a follower.

PASS THE BALL
Leaders create leaders

Hackney, London, 2002

A local resident was having problems with petty crime. A gang was breaking into his car, a rather pretty Saab 900 Turbo. Every time he changed the locks, the car was broken into again. One day he decided not to lock it – and so the gang began to use the car as a toilet. In despair, he approached the local police. 'What are you going to do about it?' he demanded. 'We don't have the resources,' the constable replied. 'What are *you* going to do about it?'

Teenage Kicks was born.

A five-a-side football tournament for disaffected youth, the purpose of Teenage Kicks was simple yet powerful: to turn gangs into teams.

In a community suffering from no jobs and nothing to do, the idea was to create a structure of meaning: a sense of purpose, belonging, teamwork and, most importantly, personal responsibility. It relied on a concept called 'Pass the Ball', defined as 'enabling and empowering the individual by entrusting them with responsibility for the success of the team'.

It worked like this.

The organizers took care of the venue, the referees, the equipment, the stewards and the schedule, and then set about handing over responsibility – passing the ball – to the area's disaffected youth.

They targeted existing gang members, and those likely to fall into the gang lifestyle. The first targets were alpha males, aged between nineteen and twenty-five, who displayed qualities of natural leadership; courage, respect, and the ability to involve and motivate others.

These natural leaders were invited to become Managers – a role that resonated in a community sandwiched about halfway between Arsenal and Tottenham Hotspur Football Clubs. The Manager's first responsibility was to find a Captain for their team – to pass the ball to them. And the Captain's first responsibility? To pick a team.

And the teams' responsibility?

To turn up for every game on time. If they didn't the team was disqualified; not just from that game, but from the whole tournament.

In this way the responsibility was passed on and caught by everyone involved.

Perhaps a dozen teams were expected to turn up on the first night. Fifty-two teams arrived on time and ready to play. Over the next four weeks no team was disqualified.

Ten years later, Teenage Kicks is still going strong.

Pass the ball.

~

'The management always felt,' says Graham Henry, 'that they had to transfer the leadership from senior management members to the players . . . they play the game and they have to do the leading on the field. The traditional "you and them" became "us".'

Leadership groups were formed, giving key senior players a distinct portfolio of responsibilities from on-field leadership to social organization, new-player mentoring to community relations. The players 'induct those [young] players, tell them what the expectations are,' says Henry. 'It's better coming from their peers.'

> Leaders create leaders by passing on responsibility, creating ownership, accountability and trust.

Under Henry's command, and with Enoka facilitating, the group began the patient process of culture change. 'With that responsibility and privilege comes *mana*,' says Enoka, 'so it's not an oppressive thing.' It didn't happen overnight, and by their own reckoning, they didn't get it right straightaway, but slowly the culture change began to take effect.

The structure of the working week epitomizes this management model: the Sunday evening review meetings are facilitated by the coaches, though significant input comes from the on-field leadership. Then over the course of the week, you see a gradual handing over of responsibility and decision-making.

By Thursday, the priorities, intensity levels and other aspects are all 'owned' by the players. By the time they play on Saturday the players have taken over the asylum.

'I'm just a resource,' says Henry.

This can clearly be translated into business, where the leader sets objectives and parameters, then 'passes the ball' to the team, handing over responsibility for implementation and detail. Leading by creating leaders.

Unlike other international teams, the All Blacks aren't given a rousing team talk by the coaches before the match. As Henry tells a Rugby World Cup press conference, 'the time before they run out on the field, is their time. It has to be their time. They've got to set their own minds right and settled and on the job.' He says that enabling his players to take charge of their own environment is, of all his achievements in rugby, the thing of which he is most proud.

> Shared responsibility means shared ownership. A sense of inclusion means individuals are more willing to give themselves to a common cause.

'We had to grow more collaborative, so that together we grow,' says Gilbert Enoka, 'together we advance.'

'We changed totally from unilateral decision making to dual management and the players had a big part of setting the standards, the life standards, the behaviours that are acceptable,' Wayne Smith says.

'Dual leadership was a very important part of our success,' says Graham Henry. 'Perhaps the reason for that success.'

Pass the ball.

~

'Leaders don't create followers,' Tom Peters famously wrote, 'they create more leaders.' In a recent Annual Wharton Leadership Conference presentation, astronaut Jeffrey S. Ashby and adventurer John Kanengieter discussed the importance of 'active followers'. Both gave examples of situations when, under pressure, one or more of their team had 'stepped up' and taken responsibility for a crucial part of a project. 'Our leadership model leverages the strength of active followers,' says Kanengieter, 'which is highly effective during uncertainty and times of conflicting options.'

Yet according to Saatchi's Kevin Roberts, even this doesn't go far enough:

——— *Language is pivotal to winning, language sets the mental and the physical frame for victory . . . A team of 'followers' is immediately on the back foot. A team of leaders steps up and finds a way to win.*

In the book *All In: The Education of General David Petraeus*, the former commander of US forces in Afghanistan, says, 'Instill in your team members a sense of great self-worth – that each, at any given time, can be the most important on the battlefield.'

In 2011, Stephen Donald became an unlikely hero.

A year before, Donald had played what many thought would be his last game as an All Black, after an unfortunate performance against Australia. As the Rugby World Cup unfolded on the world stage, he was fishing up the Waikato River.

But then a series of disasters hit the All Blacks.

Dan Carter, the fly-half – arguably the most talented player in the world; unarguably the highest point scorer in history – was considered essential for an All Blacks victory. During a final kicking practice, he felt a pop and then the pain. Carter had torn a tendon and his Rugby World Cup was over. A nation wept.

Second to go was his understudy, Colin Slade. In the quarter final against Argentina, he aggravated a groin injury, and was out. A nation mourned.

Meanwhile, with only one specialist fly-half left in the squad, Graham Henry tracked down Donald's mobile phone number and, when Donald eventually called him back, the coach asked what he was doing – whitebaiting. 'We'd had a good day, hauling in around 11 kilos, but it got a lot better,' Donald later told a crowded RWC press conference. Henry told him that if he brought his haul to the Heritage Hotel in Auckland, he'd be in the All Blacks squad.

In the forty-third minute of the final against France, the third-choice playmaker, Aaron Cruden, fell to the ground, his knee hyper-extended. Yesterday's man, Stephen Donald, ran on to the pitch, his borrowed black jersey a size or two small. A nation stopped breathing.

In the tightest and most gruelling of finals, the French gave away a penalty. Without needing to be being asked, and with destiny hanging on the moment, Donald stepped up, nodded at the goalposts, and landed the kick.

They proved to be the winning points.

New Zealand's fourth choice fly-half, having not played a game of rugby for six weeks, stood up when it counted and became a leader on the day.

Pass the ball.

~

When Henry explains that 'the traditional way no longer works', he is referring to the old-school, centralized command structure that seeks to micromanage, from above, every detail of a project. The problem in a VUCA world is that its effectiveness is limited. In his book, *Delivering Results*, human resources guru David Ulrich quotes General Gordon R. Sullivan, former Chief of Staff to the US Army.

_____ *The competitive advantage is nullified when you try to run decisions up and down the chain of command. All platoons and tank crews have real-time information on what is going on around them, the location of the enemy, and the nature and targeting of the enemy's weapons system. Once the commander's intent is understood, decisions must be devolved to the lowest possible level to allow these front line soldiers to exploit the opportunities that develop.*

In this VUCA world we all live in – whether military, business or sport – teams need to be able to respond more quickly, revise tactics and make decisions in the field.

In his white paper *'America's Military – A Profession of Arms'*, General Martin E. Dempsey, Chairman of the Joint Chiefs of Staff, lays out the framework for the future of military command – one designed to deal with asymmetric, real-time battle situations. It is called 'mission command', which replaces the old top-down hierarchy of 'command & control' in which soldiers on the ground were just pawns:

_____ *The increasing complexity and uncertainty anticipated in the future environment demand that Joint Force 2020 employ mission command to unleash its full potential in a way that harnesses the initiative and innovation of all members of the team. Leaders must empower individual initiative by providing clear, concise, and complete mission orders in a climate of mutual trust and understanding.*

The mission command model requires the leader to provide:

1. A clearly defined goal
2. The resources
3. The time-frame

The rest is up to the individuals in the field. A clear understanding of the leader's intention, and the right training are key to the implementation of mission command.

Former heavyweight champion of the world Mike Tyson said, 'Everyone has a plan until they're punched in the face.' Mission command is a response to a VUCA world in which everything that can go wrong will go wrong.

By arming staff with intention, leaders can enable their people to respond appropriately to changing context, without losing sight of the tactical imperative.

Tested and refined in the field, mission command has been proven to:

- Develop autonomous, critical thinkers able to Observe, Orient, Decide and Act, and adjust their actions on the run.
- Facilitate an adaptive environment, enabling good decision making under pressure.
- Create flexible leadership groups – developing individuals who can step in with clarity, certainty and autonomy.
- Create a sense of 'ownership' within the team; building trust and a common understanding.
- Create a decision framework; marking out roles, responsibilities and response so decision-making is intuitive, instantaneous and delivers on intention.

Henry, Smith, Hansen and Enoka – alongside the rest of the All Blacks' leadership – 'operationalized' this in key ways. They:

- Made an active decision to change and formed a powerful sense of purpose for the team.
- Devolved leadership to senior players by forming a Leadership Group, entrusting its members with key decisions and authority to enforce standards and behaviours.
- Developed individual operating units, in which each player had a specific portfolio of responsibility and leadership.
- Structured their weeks so that responsibility for decision making gradually evolved from management towards

players; by Saturday the team was entirely in the hands of the players.

° Created a 'Train to Win' system – preparing the team under pressure using randomized problem-solving techniques, active questioning and high-intensity training to prepare them for the heat of competition.

° Focused on an understanding of how the brain reacts to stress to provide the tools to help players stay present, connected, clear and accurate in order to make better decisions under pressure.

° Created a 'learning environment' dedicated to developing the individual in a tailored, self-managed programme of self-improvement.

° Developed techniques, rituals and language that connected players to the core; using storytelling in all its forms to create a sense of purpose and intention.

Pass the ball.

~

In 2004, there was a 'direct assault on the leadership' says Anton Oliver. 'They had to completely deconstruct what they were looking at. It showed a lot of courage from Graham Henry, because he's a control freak, right? But the success of the team is all on the back of the questions that he asked himself.'

Henry displays what Jim Collins, in *Good to Great*, calls

> Leaders create leaders. They arm their subordinates with intent. And then step out of the way.

Level 5 Leadership, a 'paradoxical blend of personal humility and professional will'. It didn't come naturally to Henry – an instinctive autocrat. But his maturation enabled him to create a collaborative culture in which individual talents could rise and flourish, and in which Stephen Donald could step up under pressure, make good decisions and execute with accuracy.

In *Good to Great*, Collins identifies a fact that should be remembered by non-executive board members everywhere:

_____ *all good-to-great companies had Level 5 Leadership at the time of transition*

Level 5 leaders, Collins argues, 'channel their ego needs away from themselves and into the larger goal of building a great company. Their ambition is first and foremost for the institution, not themselves.'

Pass the ball.

Pass the Ball

Enlightened leaders deliberately hand over responsibility in order to create engaged team-players able to adapt their approach to suit the conditions. 'Command & Control' in a VUCA world is unwieldy and increasingly uncompetitive. By creating a devolved management structure, leaders create ownership, autonomy and initiative. Arming their people with intent, they visualize the end-state, outline the plan, provide the right resources and trust their people to deliver. The result is a team of individuals prepared and able to stand up when it counts – leaders in the field.

Pass the Ball

Leaders create leaders.

_____ *Ki ngā whakaeke haumi.*

Join those who can join the sections of a canoe.

(Look for a leader who can bring people together.)

V

LEARN

_____ *Kohia te kai rangatira, ruia te taitea.*
Gather the good food, cast away the rubbish.

CREATE A LEARNING
ENVIRONMENT
Leaders are teachers

'I'm from an educational background', says Graham Henry. 'So I'm very keen on it being a learning environment. The result of this is that people get better, they're always improving ... how can we make this better, how can we improve this?'

~

In *Drive*, Daniel Pink lists the three factors that he believes creates motivation in a human being: mastery, autonomy and purpose.

Purpose is the connection to the core identity of the team, as discussed in Chapter II; it creates a shared emotional connection between a group of people and is a stronger motivator than money, status or a new company car.

Autonomy is the direct result of the dual leadership/ mission command model discussed in Chapter IV; it comes from team members having control over their own destiny, the choice of how they respond to a given task and a sense of self-determination.

Mastery is the subject of this chapter.

The key questions are 'How do leaders create an environment that delivers the opportunity for personal growth and professional development?' 'How do they enable mastery?' And, 'How do they make it happen every day?'

"

Sean Fitzpatrick is undisputedly a great All Black, perhaps the greatest. He was capped ninety-two times, played in the 1987 Rugby World Cup winning side, and captained the side from 1992 to 1997, leading them most famously to a series win against South Africa in South Africa.

He is also a student of success; his motivational company, Front Row Leadership, is constantly busy. His message: 'Be the best that you can possibly be.'

Success, he says, is 'modest improvement, consistently

done'. For him, it is about an unrelenting focus on the big goals – winning and leaving a legacy – but also constant attention to the details of practice and preparation. 'The best sports people in the world practice more than they play,' he tells *New Zealand Management Magazine*. 'Business people should practice too. They should go home at night and analyse their day's performance. They don't and they need to. To be good at something takes practice, and lots of it.'

> Excellence is a process of evolution, of cumulative learning, of incremental improvement.

'Excellent firms don't believe in excellence,' wrote Tom Peters in *Thriving on Chaos*, 'only in constant improvement and constant change.' He argues that success is the result of a long-term commitment to improving excellence – the small steps leading to a mighty leap.

'We're always challenging the status quo,' says Graham Henry. 'Always challenging the way we do things, both as an individual and as a team – how can we do things better?' In fact, one of the pillars of the All Blacks environment is that it is devoted to learning; the management are students of the game, constantly looking for the edge.

Leaders are teachers, and Henry is a teacher by trade. His educational background helped shape the All Blacks environment.

Alfred Chandler, the Pulitzer Prize business historian, once wrote that 'structure follows strategy'. That is, new organizational forms are the result of strategic imperatives. It follows that you can have all the will in the world but without the right structure in place, your strategy won't be successful. Moreover, the wrong structure will deliver, de facto, the wrong strategy.

In order to deliver the strategy encapsulated by 'Better

People Make Better All Blacks', Henry & Co. began to redesign the structure of the working week:

Sunday	Morning: injury clinic
	Late morning: recovery session
	Evening: Leadership Group planning session
Monday	Mental session and light training
Tuesday	Gym session: heavy weights
	Technical and set-piece session
Wednesday	Day off: unwind and refresh
Thursday	Morning: technical alignment
	Afternoon: intense 'train to win' sessions
Friday	Captain's run (player-led session)
Saturday	Afternoon: 'walkthrough' – closed technical session
	Evening: play

Within this overall structure, a worksheet was put in place for every individual player. This is where thought became reality and vision became action.

'Each player,' Henry says, 'had their player profile, or independent personal profile, made up of seven or eight major pillars, and that translated into a daily map of self-improvement. And that daily map of self-improvement was "Things I Do Today".'

> Enlightened leadership promotes a structured system for the development of the team, combined with a tailored map for the development of the individual.

The structure for the week – and the structuring of each player's activities and focus during that week – delivered the strategy.

And the strategy helped deliver a little gold cup.

~

The All Blacks have an advantage over most business teams. They play most weeks. The feedback is immediate – on the scoreboard and the next day in newspaper headlines. Analytics can break down the exact effectiveness of each individual in delivering the strategy. There is video replay. In business, leaders rarely have such defined parameters or immediate measurement.

Perhaps as a consequence, few businesses structure their working week as carefully or as effectively as the All Blacks. If they did, a Monday morning review over coffee and crois- sants might become a discussion about a more detailed, personal pathway: 'a map of self improvement . . . a living document,' as Henry calls it. Few companies really interrogate the connec- tion between strategy and structure, between an overall vision and the actions that take place over a working week; but with the transparency, metrics and human connectivity that are now available through technology, there are many more opportuni- ties to do this.

Gilbert Enoka has another life apart from his work as the All Blacks mental skills coach. In the off-season, he works for a large, multinational real estate firm, developing their team culture and mindset. The techniques he uses transfer from the All Blacks to the company, and vice versa.

There are, he says, tremendous 'synergies between the values, the vision and values based culture', and also in the approach to individualized development.

In both situations, 'if you don't get the kills, mate, you're out . . .'

Many of the questions he asks at the company are the same as those asked in the All Blacks set-up:

_____ *Where is the soul of this company? What is Harcourt's all about? . . . what are the values that drive your behaviour? . . . we came up with People First – they're always important . . . So doing the right thing became important, being courageous at a micro level, and encouragement at a micro level, us going into new areas, and fun and laughter. And those values . . . underlie everything and are the soul of the company. And it's all about learning.*

'Just because it's common sense,' he says of the process, 'doesn't mean it's common practice.'

Done right, the structuring of a learning system applies across multiple organizational levels. In the All Blacks set-up, it is blocked out around the season and also each test series – a 'chapter' in the overall story. The system is engineered towards optimum performance at the right time on both a team and individual basis: knowing when to introduce new players, when to rest others; the introduction and repetition of skills; and bringing the team to its physical and psychological peak at just the right time.

All this is part of rugby's inbuilt four-year cycle.

'The World Cup was a vision for years,' Henry says, 'and it came a bit clearer two years out.' Various competitions, Henry says, 'were the stepping-stones to winning and having improvement . . . There's a structure there of team improvement, just like there's a structure there of individual improvement, which is ongoing.'

And then there is 'a set of programmes you use to try and do the business on the paddock,' says Graham Henry. 'Although there's a set routine, a set ritual of preparation . . . little things

come in to add a bit of icing to that – a little bit of edge to that.'
This 'edge' includes the psychological incentive to beat this team on this particular day, because the opposition is Australia or England, or because a player is winning his fiftieth cap.

> A map of daily self-improvement acts as a powerful tool to develop teams and organizations; this 'living document' provides fresh goals and develops new skills so people push themselves harder, become more capable and achieve more for the team.

'The edge is better,' Henry says, smiling.

Leaders are teachers.

~

The All Blacks display an institutionalized system of continuous improvement, one that works on the super-structural level (the season and the four-year World Cup cycle), the team level (selection, the tapering of performance, tactical preparation, etc), and the individual level ('Things I Do Today'). And like the original meaning of *kaizen*, it begins with self-empowerment; developing the individual's ability to stand up and take the lead when called upon.

But it goes one step further.

It becomes about the sporting buzz-phrase *du jour* – 'the aggregation of marginal gains' or 'the drive to perfect every controllable detail in search of optimal performance'.

'Races are won by a fraction of a second,' wrote John Wooden. 'National Championship games by a single point. That fraction of a second or a single point is the result of relevant details performed along the way.'

Marginal gains have been made famous in recent times through the work of Clive Woodward with his England rugby squad and Dave Brailsford with British Cycling and Team Sky.

When Woodward took over the England rugby team in 1997 he inherited an archaic parallel universe in which the coach didn't have a desk at Rugby House and, despite a huge advantage in player numbers and finances, England were, in Graham Henry's memorable phrase, 'world champions at wasting talent'.

Woodward brought in Humphrey Walters, a consultant who ran a 'learning and development' company called MaST International. Together, they set out to effect wholesale culture change, restructuring the players' experience 'from driveway to driveway'. That is, from the moment the English players left home to play for their country to the moment they returned, everything would be considered, analysed and aligned with the team's values, purpose and strategy.

This meant deep and expensive structural changes of personnel, training venues and the organizational relationship between the team and its employers, even the way the team travelled to games. 'You can't,' Walters told Woodward, 'fire a cannon out of a canoe.'

According to Woodward (in his book, *Winning*), Walters taught him 'that success can be attributed to how a team worked together under pressure, how they understood the importance of team work and loyalty, and how they were willing to do a hundred things just 1% better'.

This final aspect Woodward called 'the critical non-essentials'. A fresh jersey at halftime, the same | Leaders are learners.

bus for every game, a more inspiring locker room at Twickenham – every little thing helped Woodward's England win the 2003 Rugby World Cup.

Britain's Olympic cyclists called it 'marginal gains'. In their preparation for a home Olympics in 2012, in which they won an incredible seven out of ten gold medals, the details included:

- customized aerodynamic helmets
- 'hot pants' – worn to keep thigh muscles warm between races
- sweat-resistant clothing
- alcohol sprayed on wheels to enhance traction at the start
- hypoallergenic pillows to help stop riders catching colds

At Team Sky, it also involved transporting Bradley Wiggins's bed throughout the 2,173-mile, twenty-three-day course of the Tour de France, over the Channel to London, up to his home for a break in Lancashire, and back down to London again for the Olympics.

Sometimes the small things can take a big effort. And cost a lot of money.

'The whole principle,' Brailsford explains to the BBC, 'came from the idea that if you broke down everything you could think of that goes into riding a bike, and improved it by 1 per cent, you will get a significant increase when you put it all together.'

At McLaren F1, they call it 'Tenths'. The entire team is galvanized by the idea of shaving tenths of a second off the lap time. All F1 teams do it, of course, but at McLaren they make it their central operating principle.

Marginal gain can be technical, physical, practical, operational, and even psychological. In the film *Any Given Sunday*, the Al Pacino character calls it 'Inches':

———— *You find out that life is just a game of inches. So is football. Because in either game, life or football, the margin for error is so small . . . On this team, we fight for that inch. On this team, we tear ourselves, and everyone around us to pieces for that inch . . . Cause we know when we add up all those inches that's going to make the fucking difference between WINNING and LOSING.*

'We talked about a learning environment,' says Graham Henry, 'and everyone getting better and everyone getting bigger every day, so if each player improves by 5 per cent minimum, 10 per cent, 15 per cent, the team's going to improve. If you put these collective percentages together you've got something special.'

> Marginal gains: 100 things done 1 per cent better to deliver cumulative competitive advantage.

~

Creating a learning environment demands that leaders step back and look at their team, business or organization as what engineers call a closed or bound system: with a defined parameter in which every input is known. Though it's clearly easier to define parameters around an elite sports team, for any team it is important to understand where the team boundaries begin and where they end. It's basic border control

'You are a product of your environment,' says author W. Clement Stone, 'so choose the environment that will best develop you towards your objective. Analyze your life in terms of your environment. Are the things around you helping you towards success – or are they holding you back?' After all, 'It's not the mountains ahead that wear you out,' said Muhammad Ali, 'it's the pebble in your shoe.'

By working hard to control the environment, the All Blacks seek to eliminate the pebbles in their shoes.

Saying yes to high performance means first saying no. 'When you look at the rituals, for instance,' says Gilbert Enoka, 'what we've actually done . . . is to strip things out . . . What hasn't changed are the "go-tos" that drive the legacy . . . the art is knowing what to spit out.'

'People think focus means saying yes to the thing you've got to focus on,' Apple founder Steve Jobs told the writer Walter Isaacson, 'but that's not what it means at all. It means saying no to the hundred other good ideas that are there. You've got to pick carefully.'

In the England set-up under Woodward, Humphrey Walters likened it to taking all the furniture out of a house – all the chairs and tables and fixtures and fittings, and the mysterious stuff that accumulates in drawers – and only putting back what is useful.

This is as much about controlling the psychological environment as it is the physical. Computer programmers have a phrase: Garbage In/Garbage Out. If we apply the analogy, this means:

- the verbal, visual and gestural language that we allow to take up residence in our heads;
- the toxins like alcohol, drugs or sugar that we allow to take up residence in our bodies (and minds);
- the people we allow to take up space in our lives.

Psychologists talk about stimulus response – whether it's the influence certain people have on us, or certain substances have on our metabolism, we must be careful what we ingest.

We have to be careful what furniture we reintroduce to our metaphorical house. Key to a high-performing learning environment is the quality of the material that is allowed to enter – to permeate our 'bound system' and become the stimulus for our response.

The All Blacks are notoriously judicious in eliminating undue influence; equally, they are curious and innovative when it comes to seeking out stimuli, knowledge and insights from other people and organizations.

Coaches Henry, Smith and Hansen have visited other teams – the New York Giants, Sydney Swans, Melbourne Storm, among others – to better understand their culture, standards and systems. The All Blacks mantra 'No Dickheads' was shamelessly stolen from the Sydney Swans.

Scrum coach Mike Cron is also a student of sport. 'Part of my NZ contract allows me to go anywhere in the world to upskill myself,' he told the *Samoa Times*. 'I've been to sumo wrestling camps in Japan, judo camp in Japan, the NY Knicks, Yankees and Giants, NFL camp in Florida to pick up ideas.'

The team brought in an eye-coach who introduced them to various exercises to improve spatial awareness, and psychiatrists and Karate black belts to work on the All Blacks' untimely habit of crumbling under World Cup pressure. Enoka also brought in the wisdom of Māori artist and *kapa haka* exponent, Derek Lardelli, to help reconnect the team to their identity and develop a new *haka* – '*Kapo O Panga*' – to express their sense of self.

Like all good teachers the All Blacks coaches are students, not only of the game but also of human nature. Like all good teachers, they love to learn.

~

In the run-up to the Rugby World Cup, the coaches brought in a man called Jock Hobbs to address the team.

'A fabulous man,' says Graham Henry, 'and a sad situation.' Hobbs was a former All Blacks captain and, until illness forced him to stand down, CEO of the NZRU. He had leukaemia, a condition that has since claimed his life.

He spoke to the team about the inspiring effect they were having on the country, and about his personal challenges and how they related to the team.

'Get up every day and be the best you can be,' he said. 'Be the best in the world. . . . give your all for every second of every minute of the seven games you'll play. You can do no more than that. Guys, never let the music die in you.'

Leaders are teachers.

Another speaker was a man called Willie Apiata, a recipient of the Victoria Cross, the highest award for gallantry. His medal citation for the action, which took place in a remote valley in Afghanistan, reads:

_____ *In total disregard of his own safety, Lance Corporal Apiata stood up and lifted his comrade bodily. He then carried him across the seventy metres of broken, rocky and fire-swept ground, fully exposed in the glare of battle to heavy enemy fire . . . Having delivered his wounded companion to relative shelter [he] re-armed himself and rejoined the fight in counter-attack.*

His message about playing for the team and relying on each other – 'otherwise you die' – was clear. At the end, Graham Henry says, 'the All Blacks stood up and gave a standing ovation to Willie and Willie was clapping the All Blacks. They both had the utmost respect.'

'The environment that people live in,' wrote nineteenth-century chemist Ellen Swallow Richards, 'is the environment they learn to live in, respect and perpetuate.'

When the environment is dedicated to learning, the score, as Bill Walsh says, takes care of itself. Leaders are teachers – our job is to lead people through uncertainty and confusion and into self-knowledge and self-possession. 'The ability to help the people around me self-actualize their goals,' says Walsh, 'underlies the single aspect of my abilities and the label that I value most – teacher.'

Sometimes it only takes one encounter – one teacher – to change a life, and many lives after that.

> Successful leaders look beyond their own field to discover new approaches, learn best practices and push the margins. Then they pass on what they have learned.

~

Sean Fitzpatrick's teacher was a man called Guy Davis, who was coaching Fitzpatrick's lower grade rugby team. As Fitzpatrick writes in *Winning Matters*, he changed the young player's life forever.

He told the future All Blacks captain that 'it didn't matter what level of talent had been given to us, what size we were or how fast or slow we ran. It was what we did with that talent that we had that counted . . . no excuses and no exceptions. "The only thing I want you to be is the best that you can possibly be."'

It's a lesson Fitzpatrick has carried with him all his life and passes on to all he meets.

'What you leave behind is not what is engraved in stone monuments,' said the Greek statesman Pericles, 'but what is woven into the lives of others.' Your legacy is that which you teach.

Create a Learning Environment

Human beings are motivated by purpose, autonomy and a drive towards mastery. Accomplished leaders create an environment in which their people can develop their skills, their knowledge and their character. This leads to a learning environment and a culture of curiosity, innovation and continuous improvement. By finding the 100 things that can be done just 1 per cent better, leaders create incremental and cumulative advantage, and organizations see an upswing in performance and results. In creating a coherent learning environment, it pays to both eliminate unhelpful elements – clearing out the furniture – and to introduce insightful and inspiring influences.

Create a Learning Environment

Leaders are teachers.

Te Tīmatanga o te mātauranga ko te wahangū,
te wāhanga tuarua ko te whakarongo.
The first stage of learning is silence,
the second stage is listening.

VI

WHĀNAU

_____ *Ā muri kia mau ki te kawau mārō, whanake ake, whanake ake.*

Hold to the spearhead formation of the *kawau*.

NO DICKHEADS
Follow the spearhead

Taranaki, New Zealand

A flock of birds – *kawau*, a kind of cormorant – carve a graceful V across the breaking day. One bird leads, another follows, another takes the lead, in an endless synchronized support system, much like the peloton of professional cyclists.

Ornithologists say that flying this way is 70 per cent more efficient than flying solo. If a bird falls out of formation, it feels the wind resistance and rejoins the flock. Should one fall behind, others stay back until it can fly again. No bird gets left behind.

It is an extraordinary organizational dynamic – and the perfect metaphor for the Māori concept of *whānau*.

Whānau means to 'be born' or 'give birth'.

For Māori, it means extended family: parents, grand-parents, uncles, aunts, children and cousins. In the vernacular, it has come to mean our family of friends: our mates, our tribe, our team.

In Māori mythology, *whānau* is symbolized by a spearhead, an image derived in turn from the flight formation of the kawau. A spearhead has three tips – but to work properly, all the force must move in one direction.

And so it is with *whānau*.

For a *whānau* to function, everyone must move towards the same point. You are free to choose the course you take, but the spearhead is most effective if you all work together.

Fly in formation. Be of one mind. Follow the spearhead.

This is the 'being of team' and the essence of the successful organization.

'We need people who will work hard and work hard for their

brother,' says Gilbert Enoka. 'We know that is a pretty good formula – because that way you get contribution.'

The definition of a great team, says Kevin Roberts, the global CEO of Saatchi & Saatchi, is one that is 'in flow more frequently than the opposition'. For collective flow to occur, he believes, organizations must be of 'one mind'.

The legendary Phil Jackson, former head coach of the Chicago Bulls basketball team, calls this the 'Group Mind' and it was the basis of his extraordinary coaching career. When Jackson first brought Michael Jordon to Chicago, he was the league's top scorer in each of his first six seasons, far and away the best player in the NBA, yet he had never won a title.

'A great player can only do so much on his own,' said Jackson in his book *Sacred Hoops*. 'No matter how breathtaking his one-on-one moves, if he is out of sync psychologically with everyone else, the team will never achieve the harmony needed to win a championship.'

'This is the struggle that every leader faces,' Jackson says. 'How to get members of the team who are driven by the quest for individual glory to give themselves over wholeheartedly to the group effort.'

Jackson would quote Rudyard Kipling:

> *For the Strength of the Pack is the Wolf,*
> *and the strength of the Wolf is the Pack.*

'On a good team there are no superstars,' Jackson's mentor, Red Holzman, taught him. 'There are great players who show they are great players by being able to play with others as a team . . . they make sacrifices; they do things necessary to help the team win.'

The results of Jackson's egoless approach speak for themselves. When Michael Jordon retired in 2003 he had won six championship rings and was voted Most Valuable Player in all of those finals. Turning his 'me' into a 'we' had alchemized his reputation into trophies and medals. Being a great team player made him a great player, the greatest of all time.

> The strength of the wolf is the pack.

~

'It's everything in a team, to be honest,' says All Black legend Andrew Mehrtens. 'It's about thinking about the team's interest before yourself . . . if it's not good for the team, don't say it and don't do it.'

'We've all got our certain role to play,' he says, 'and if you can have that respect within the group, then you are going to go a lot further . . . if the guy like a goal kicker can respect the ability, the difficulty, of the guy throwing into the lineout, or how tough it is for a guy to hold in the scrum on the right-hand side . . .'

~

Owen Eastwood says that if the first steps in developing a high performance culture are to:

1. select on character,
2. understand your strategy for change,
3. co-write a purpose,
4. devolve leadership and
5. encourage a learning environment.

The sixth and arguably most important step is to begin to turn the standards into action. The best way of doing this is through peer-to-peer enforcement. 'Respect as a value is vague,' says Eastwood, 'but has impact when players decide this means no phones in meetings, no talking over each other, etc. Values alone risk becoming wallpaper and meaningless.' But, he adds, 'defining and enforcing these standards needs to be from bottom up.'

'These are young guys, they are on television, they've got lots of money, they've never had it before, birds are after them,' says Anton Oliver, 'but if you're not reflecting the team culture ... boys will fuck you.'

The strength of the wolf is the pack.

It used to be called 'the back seat of the bus', the natural hierarchy that developed within an All Blacks side and which was most easily seen in the seating arrangement on the team coach: senior players at the back, rookies up at the front; non-All Blacks strictly not welcome.

The senior members of the team would enforce the standards, because they were *their* standards. In the old days, this was also seen in the Sunday Court Sessions, where senior players would hand down fines, mostly liquid, usually instant. But the world had moved on and, as the All Blacks management began to actively encourage peer-to-peer enforcement, the standards quickly went from the back of the bus to the front of the mind.

In its simplest form, this involved the mentoring of younger players by the senior figures. It involved the Leadership Group in collective decision making in areas such as: community appearances, advertising approvals and which charity the team would support. It also involved the Leadership Group being left (and trusted) to sort out internal problems within the team.

This came into play most vividly during the Rugby World Cup when two players, Cory Jane and Israel Dagg, decided to have a big night in a Takapuna Bar. The next day, as radio commentators screamed for their scalps, the sheepish pair were brought before the seven most senior players and asked to explain themselves. For young men, at the prime of their lives, in the tournament of their dreams, this must have been both mortifying and humbling. Later, they made a public apology to the rest of the team and the case was closed.

As Bob Howitt writes:

_____ *This is a classic example of the dual management struc-ture operating within the team: a lecture from a grumpy manager wouldn't have had half the same impact of the two players as facing their peers had. Young men hate letting their peers and team mates down, on or off the field.*

Both players would go on to play prominent roles in the semi-final win against Australia.

~

'For everyone to go in the same direction,' says Andrew Mehrtens, 'you've got to have strong links in the team. If there are weak links then you will have guys going off in different directions and that's no good for anyone.'

Which is why Wayne Smith invented the 'Rugby Club'.

'The All Blacks,' he explains, 'are the most privileged club in the world . . . It's a place you have to earn your way into and it's hugely exclusive.

> The being of team begins from inside. High standards must come from within. Leadership works best when your team takes the lead.

'I really felt that the Rugby Club would give us an opportunity for players to talk about the past . . . be proud of where they come from, and who they are.'

Smith proposed to the Leadership Group the idea of a regularly scheduled social night in which players would don their club jerseys and 'have a quiet drink' together, replicating the climate and culture that originally propelled them into the sport. It was a huge success, a chance to laugh and have fun and release themselves from the pressure.

'To be able to work together, communication is the biggest thing,' says Smith. 'And I think that comes from a team that has good links from off the field . . . a team able to spend time together and talk to one another and be honest with one another. It's incredibly important.'

'You talk about handling expectation and handling pressure,' says Graham Henry. 'You talk about leaders leading; players leading. You talk about the legacy and what that means . . . But I think the other thing that was really important was the connection between people – and the greater those connections, the more resilient and the stronger we were, the better we were.'

The strength of the wolf is the pack.

As well as the bonding aspect, the Rugby Club also serves to reconnect the players with their story, their roots, their *whānau*. The old club rugby shirts remind them of where they've come from and the position they've reached, but also remind them to keep their feet on the ground.

It is a way of staying anchored, and to attach personal meaning to team purpose. And it is an excuse to have fun. 'Whilst there is a lot of pressure on them to enhance the jersey and pass it on in a better state, if you enjoy the experience it actually makes it easier to achieve that goal,' Smith says.

Fun, with a serious purpose.

To win.

The strength of the wolf is the pack.

This kind of bonding process provides social capital – that is, the intangible benefit of closeness and cooperation, which is trust. It also provides a collective intelligence, more heads being better than one. But this sense of unity can be threatened by just one person.

An old Arab proverb says:

_____ *It's better to have a thousand enemies outside the tent than one inside the tent.*

There's a similar Māori saying:

_____ *He iti wai kōwhao waka e tahuri te waka.*
A little water seeping through a small hole may swamp a canoe.

The All Blacks, meanwhile, strictly maintain the maxim they borrowed from the Sydney Swans:

_____ *No Dickheads.*

'No Dickheads' is the antidote to the leak, the bad apple, the enemy inside the tent. It extends to selection –

> No one is bigger than the team and individual brilliance does not automatically lead to outstanding results. One selfish mindset will infect a collective culture.

some of New Zealand's favourite players have never made it to All Blacks status because they are considered to be 'dickheads'; others make it but are never invited back. It's a powerful and effective philosophy that helps maintain an exceptional environment.

One disaffected or selfish individual infects the group. Remove them and the group will cohere and heal.

No Dickheads.

Setting high standards – and putting the measures in place to maintain them through peer-to-peer enforcement – is a critical component in successful team culture. In fact, all the coaches mentioned so far – Bill Walsh, Vince Lombardi, John Wooden, Phil Jackson and Clive Woodward – began their tenure by implementing a set of high, non-negotiable standards. These standards are how they identified the expectations and set the ethos, the culture, of the team.

There is tremendous overlap in their philosophies and that of the All Blacks.

Vince Lombardi says, 'as a leader you're being watched 24 hours each day'.

The All Blacks say, 'You're an All Black, 24-7.'

Bill Walsh installed 'an agenda of specific behavioural norms – actions and attitudes – that applied to every single person on our payroll'.

The All Blacks say, 'Better People Make Better All Blacks'.

Phil Jackson's goal was 'to find a structure that would empower everyone on the team, not just the stars, and allow the players to grow as individuals as they surrendered themselves to the team effort'.

The All Blacks had a dual-leadership model.

John Wooden said that a player who makes the team great is better than a great player.

The All Blacks say: 'No one is bigger than the team.'

In his book *Good to Great*, Jim Collins argues for the primacy of the 'who' before the 'what'; the 'we' before the 'me'. He quotes Ken Kesey in *The Electric Kool-Aid Acid Test*: 'You're either on the bus or off the bus.' His research shows that 'good to great leaders began by first getting the right people on the bus (and the wrong people off the bus) and then figured out where to drive it'.

He implies you don't have to be ruthless, just rigorous. As the saying goes, if you insist on only the best, you very often get it. In the All Blacks they are both rigorous and ruthless; they insist on the best and they always seem to get it.

As current coach Steve Hansen says, 'Put your hand in a glass of water. Now take it out. That's how hard it is to replace you.'

The strength of the wolf is the pack.

No Dickheads

Whānau is your family, your mates, your team, your organization. For the *whānau* to move forward, everyone within it must move in the same direction. This is the essence of team – working hard for each other, in harmony, without dissent, submerging individual ego for a greater cause. This extends to selection – No Dickheads – and the fostering of connections, trust and collaboration between all levels of the organization. In this way people work for each other, rather than for individual glory. In the All Blacks, high standards are fundamental and are enforced by the players themselves, who are trusted to do the task. Success can be traced back to the connections between members of the team and their collective character, something true of all winning organizations. Great leaders ruthlessly protect their people, encouraging connection, collaboration and collective ownership, nurturing a safe environment of trust, respect and family.

No Dickheads

Follow the spearhead.

Kia urupū tātou; kaua e taukumekume.

Let us be united, not pulling against one another.

VII

EXPECTATIONS

—— *Ko taku reo taku ohooho, ko taku reo taku māpihi mauria.*
My language is my awakening, my language is the
window to my soul.

EMBRACE
EXPECTATIONS
Aim for the
highest cloud

Sean Fitzpatrick tells the story of being at the beginning of his career, jostling for a place in the Auckland team. The problem was he couldn't hit his lineout throws, couldn't make them stick.

Andy Haden, the Auckland and All Blacks lock, wasn't impressed.

'He told me to bugger off, basically,' says Fitzpatrick. 'Luckily for me I dealt with it the right way and went away and learnt how to throw the ball in.

'It was a hard lesson, though. I didn't play for Auckland for another two years.'

~

Another story.

It's 1993, the All Blacks against the British Lions in Wellington. Despite a narrow win in the Test before, the All Blacks ran on clear favourites. And ran off humiliated.

The score: 20–7 to the Lions.

Suddenly, with the third and final Test approaching, the All Blacks were staring into the abyss – the possibility of two straight losses for the first time since 1949. The papers savaged the team.

According to Robin McConnell in his book, *Inside The All Blacks*, so did the coach, Laurie Mains. 'I have never been so bloody humiliated as to see Poms dominating an All Blacks team ... Do you accept losing a Test match? I don't ... We need guts, we need good Kiwi toughness and heart. Above all, you're All Blacks. What are you going to do about it?'

In the locker room right after the game, Fitzpatrick told his players, 'Make a mental note of the way you feel right now – and make sure you never feel that way again.'

It was a lesson in losing that had been handed down to him. 'As All Blacks,' he tells a *London Business Forum* conference, 'you're told in no uncertain terms to remember your losses more than your wins.'

It hurt Fitzpatrick worst of all – his penalty count had been higher than the rest of his team combined. Ex-All Blacks called on Fitzpatrick to resign.

Instead, he turned the pain into motivation.

The next Test, in Auckland, they won: 27-3.

It would have been too painful to lose.

'It is the fear of not doing it properly,' says Fitzpatrick, 'and what does that do? It makes you prepare properly. And all successful teams, whether it be in business or in sport, the ones who prepare properly are the ones that normally win.'

'People get scared by the phrase fear of failure,' he says, 'because they think it inhibits their performance. But, if you're actually honest with yourself, if you actually use that as a motivating factor – to prepare well and not the night before – you know, the [business] pitches that fail are the ones where the people are up at 3 o'clock in the morning preparing . . .'

'A strong dislike of not being good enough is healthy,' says Andrew Mehrtens. 'I would do anything to win, except cheating, of course. I hated losing. Really hated losing.'

'The key,' Fitzpatrick tells his audience, 'is to understand that there is a world of difference between fear of feedback or failure and harnessing that fear to positive effect.'

Embrace expectations.

~

In Nobel-Prize winner Daniel Kahneman's book *Thinking Fast and Slow*, he writes about the benefits of a fear of failure in what he calls 'Loss Aversion'. Citing research by Devon Pope and Maurice Schweitzer at the University of Pennsylvania, he discusses the 'relative strength of two motives' in the statistics of professional golfers: 'Whether the putt was easy or hard, at every distance from the hole, the players were more successful when putting for par than for a birdie.' The difference in the rate of success was 3.6 per cent.

We don't play to win, it seems, we play not to lose.

'The history of All Blacks rugby has been so successful that the expectation in New Zealand is that we win every Test,' says Graham Henry, 'and I think that is good for the team. If you didn't have that expectation, I'm sure we wouldn't reach the standards we do.'

It's a triangulated crossfire: the expectations of a nation, the expectations from teammates and coaches, and a high level of self-expectation all coming together in one massive Loss Aversion that drives them to greater sacrifice – and success – on the field.

'We have a saying,' says Fitzpatrick, 'don't be a good All Black. Be a great All Black. Don't just be satisfied to reach your targets. Go higher.'

As Jonah Lomu told Kevin Roberts, 'We hate coming second place to ourselves.'

Embrace expectations.

It is this internal benchmark that sets apart the great from the good. 'I challenge myself to be the best basketball player every moment I'm playing the game,' Michael Jordon tells *MVP.com*.

As recounted by Tony Cozier to the BBC's Sam Sheringham, Tino Best, the West Indies fast bowler, shows how it is done on his answerphone: 'This is Tino Best speaking, the fastest bowler in the world. I can't take your call right now, but I'll get back to you as soon as I've finished practising how to get faster.'

It's similar in the Royal Air Force Aerobatic Team, says

former Red Arrows pilot Justin Hughes. 'The standard you measure yourself against is high. The debriefing is fairly brutal, not in an aggressive way but in that the team measure their own standards against much higher standards than are measured externally. The public's opinion is not what we're measuring – we're measuring something way, way higher.'

In *The Real McCaw*, the All Black captain tells Greg McGee of a childhood spent in the remote reaches of Hakataramea, up the Waitaki Valley, on the edge of the earth. Specifically, he tells the story of a conversation he had with his Uncle Bigsy – one that was to change his life.

'Do you want to be an All Black?' his uncle asked.

'Oh yeah.'

So they mapped out how to do it, writing down a series of goals that included the Canterbury Under 21s, the Canterbury provincial team – and the All Blacks in 2004.

'You don't just want to be an All Black,' Uncle Bigsy told McCaw, according to the book, 'you want to be a great All Black.'

'Sign it,' he said, indicating the list. 'Sign it Great All Black.'

'G. A. B.' McCaw somewhat sheepishly wrote, before hiding the note in his room.

When the farm in Hakataramea was sold, McCaw came back to clear out his room and found the piece of paper stuck on the back of the wardrobe. He realized he'd beaten all the targets he'd set, becoming an All Black three years ahead of schedule.

> Successful leaders have high internal benchmarks. They set their expectations high and try to exceed them.

Yet things were not good. The All Blacks had just lost the Rugby World Cup quarter-final against France. McCaw's legacy was on the line, his place in the team. He hadn't yet reached his goal.

'What would a G. A. B. do?' he asked himself.

~

Muhammad Ali began calling himself the greatest before he had any real right. 'It's the repetition of affirmation that leads to belief,' he says, 'and once that belief becomes a deep conviction, things begin to happen.'

Daniel Kahneman reminds us that these affirmations don't even need to be true: 'A message, unless it is immediately rejected as a lie, will have the same effect on the associative system regardless of its reliability . . . Whether the story is true, or believable, matters little, if at all.'

By setting even the most unrealistic self-expectation, 'the aversion to the failure of not reaching the goal is much stronger (even) than the desire to reach it.' It seems that, even in Nobel Prize-winning economics, the clichés are true:

- If you can conceive, and believe, you can achieve.
- Visualize to actualize.
- Fake it till you make it.

The truth is that the story we tell about our life *becomes* the story of our life. The narrative we tell our team, business, brand, organization or family becomes the story others eventually tell about us. This internalized narrative – triggered by words, images, movement and memory – is a phenomenon popularly known as the self-fulfilling prophecy.

First defined in 1949 by Robert K. Merton as a 'false definition of the situation evoking new behaviours which make the original conception come true', the term is more commonly used these days as a kind of warning: 'He said bad things would happen and so bad things happened.' But the reverse, as shown by McCaw, is just as true; say you'll be a G. A. B. and you might just become one.

Kahneman posits two interrelated psychological observations that help explain this: Anchoring and Priming.

Anchoring is most easily understood by recalling the tricks employed by supermarkets, shysters and salespeople everywhere. 'Normally £20!' the huckster shouts. 'For you, sir, I'll give it to you for £5. Bargain!' The anchoring of perceptions – normally £20! Bargain! – makes the lower number seem cheaper.

Priming is perhaps more surprising. In 1996, John Bargh, a social psychologist from New York University, tested what is known as the ideometer effect, a reflexive response in which actions subconsciously follow thoughts. In a now legendary experiment, he gave groups of participants single-word flashcards and asked them to construct some simple sentences. Buried within some of the groups' cards were single-word synonyms for age:

_____ *Bald. Wrinkle. Grey. Arthritis. Florida. Forgetful.*

After completing their sentences, the groups – some of whom had used the age-related flashcards, and others who had not – were then asked to walk along a corridor and sign out. Which is when the real experiment began.

Their progress down the corridor was timed – and something remarkable was discovered. Those in the groups who had been working with the words connoting age – arthritis, Florida, forgetful – walked more slowly.

_____ *They.*

    Walked.

        More.

            Slowly.

The suggestion of age – just the merest idea processed on an unconscious level – led to a reflexive response that had them display the physical behaviour of the elderly.

It's called the 'Florida Effect' and, though the results are still being debated, it indicates that perhaps our sense of free will is neither free nor always wilful, but rather a response to the stimulus around us, to our physical and psychological environment; to the way our world is posited through language.

It is a response to a story.

~

In Bruce Chatwin's book, *The Songlines*, he explores the *Koori* (Australian Aboriginal) belief that as young men go walkabout, the words they chant 'sing their world into existence'. The tribal songs learned on their mother's laps and the other more sacred songs taught by their fathers in the semi-circles of Corroboree are chanted and hummed as the initiates walk their songlines. With the words they sing come images, new ancient landscapes of their mind's eye: the dream becoming the reality, the word made world.

Chatwin also reminds us that the Ancient Egyptians believed that the seat of the soul is our tongue. Using it as our rudder, and words as our oar, we steer our way across the waters to our destiny. From ancient theology to contemporary psychology, our words shape our story and this story becomes the framework for our behaviours; and our behaviours determine the way we lead our life and the way we run our organizations.

Richie McCaw tells Greg McGee that he has always kept a notebook. It's a working document, a library of affirmations, mantras, notes-to-self, reminders, exhortations, expectations, anchors and priming words.

'Need to be positive and keep belief with the boys with what we're doing.'

'Physicality is the key.'

'Positive mentality in how we're going to play.'

On game day, the first words in McCaw's book are always the same – 'Start Again' – a reminder that you have to prove yourself again, today. For McCaw, if it's not written, it's not real.

~

The truth is, we don't so much tell stories, as stories tell us.

Our narratives frame and structure our lives, becoming the prism through which we perceive and live. Ira Glass, the host of US radio show, *This American Life*, expresses it perfectly: 'Great stories happen to those who tell them.' And vice versa.

This is true for both individuals and organizations.

Dr Pamela Rutledge, Director of the Media Psychology Research Centre says:

_____ *Stories are how we think. They are how we make*
meaning of life. Call them schemas, scripts,
cognitive maps, mental models, metaphors, or narratives.
Stories are how we explain how things work,
how we make decisions, how we justify our decisions,
how we persuade others, how we understand our place
in the world, create our identities, and define and
teach social values.

This has particular relevance to leadership today, argues

John Kotter, culture-change guru and former professor at Harvard Business School:

_____ *We learn best – and change – from hearing stories that strike a chord with us . . . Those in leadership positions who fail to grasp or use the power of stories risk failure for their companies or for themselves.*

The language we use embeds itself and becomes action, so it is critical to respect it, shape it and deploy it strategically. The filmmaker Robert Rodriguez once wrote that the first step to becoming a Hollywood director is to get a business card with the word 'director' printed under your name. Apple set out to put a 'dent in the universe' and it did. Richie McCaw set out to become a Great All Black.

In the lead up to the Rugby World Cup, the All Blacks set themselves an internal challenge: 'To be the best rugby team there has ever been'.

_____ *Whāia te iti kahurangi; ki te tuohu koe,*
me he maunga teitei.
Aim for the highest cloud, so that if you miss it,
you will hit a lofty mountain.

It wasn't about boasting, in fact it was the opposite. It was the team's equivalent of G. A. B. – the highest cloud, a benchmark, what Jim Collins would call a Big Hairy Audacious Goal.

'It just became a natural part of what we did,' said Graham Henry, 'so that everyone's expectations in that group were the ultimate. And they spoke and walked that way.'

'Judge yourself against the world's best,' Sean Fitzpatrick tells his audience. 'Without question.'

Embrace Expectations

By embracing a fear of failure, we can lift our performance, using a healthy loss aversion to motivate us. Equally, it pays to hoist our sights if we aspire to be world class: to create for ourselves a narrative of extreme, even unrealistic ambition. It doesn't even matter if it's true, or reasonable, or possible; it only matters that we do it. In this way, we set our internal and team benchmarks to the ultimate. Inspiring leaders use bold, even unrealistic goals to lift their game and the power of story-telling to 'sing their world into existence'. They tell great, vivid, epic stories of what is possible to themselves and their teams – and soon the world repeats the story back to them.

Embrace Expectations

Aim for the highest cloud.

_____ *Kia whakangawari au i a hau.*

Let us prepare ourselves for the fray.

VIII

PREPARATION

_____ *Ko te piko o te māhuri, tērā te tupu o te rākau.*
The way the sapling is shaped determines
how the tree grows.

TRAIN TO WIN
Practise under
pressure

Shepherd St, Bowral, New South Wales, Australia, 1915

A different sport; another lesson.

A small boy is playing cricket alone in a backyard. The sound of ball on bat echoes over the neighbourhood, rebounding over ordinary weatherboard bungalows in an ordinary Australian town.

The bat is a cricket stump. The ball is a golf ball.

The boy throws the ball against a curved, corrugated wall. Each time he throws, it flies off at a different, random angle.

Sometimes he cuts. Sometimes he blocks. Sometimes he drives.

Every time, though, he hits the ball.

Every time.

The boy does this every morning, every afternoon, every day and every year for a decade. In his first game for the local school, aged twelve, he scores 115 not out. In the return match his captain retires him on 72. For the third match the opposing captain refuses to field a team if he is selected.

A few years later, during his first season of club cricket, the boy scores 995 runs in just nine innings. In 1927 he plays his first first-class match.

The next year he plays for his country. Twenty years later he retires, with an average Test score of 99.94 – dismissed one run short of an extraordinary career average of 100.

The boy's name was Donald Bradman, the finest sportsman of any generation.

Bradman learned his trade on the backstreets of Bowral by bouncing a golf ball off a corrugated wall and hitting it back with a cricket stump.

He made practice his test.

~

'Practise with intensity to develop the mindset to win,' the All Blacks say. It's a methodology called 'Train to Win' and Graham Henry describes it as one of the key strategic pillars that propelled his team to World Cup victory.

'We talked about leadership and expectation, a learning environment and those sorts of things; we were handling pressure . . . and that involved a lot of pretty simple brain biology and how the brain works under stress and how you handle that stress.'

'The training, decision-making wise, should be harder than the game,' says Wayne Smith. 'So you try an overlying principle of throwing problems at them – unexpected events – forcing them to solve the problems.'

Like Bradman's corrugated wall.

Patrick McKendry in the *New Zealand Herald* described the final full training session before an All Blacks match:

_____ *Training on Thursday is all about intensity. The players don't stop for mistakes as they once did. They reason, quite rightly, that opposition teams don't stop for All Blacks' errors – they try to take advantage of them – so they should train that way.*

'We wanted to replicate playing conditions,' says Smith. 'I used to constantly try and put [scrum-half] Jimmy Cowen under pressure by telling him they were going to score against him at training . . . to replicate what it was going to be like on the field.'

He explains: 'By throwing all sorts of problem-solving situations at them and randomizing situations, we found we were getting better long-term learning. If you are not over-extending yourself you're not going to get much learning . . . there's no point in ducking the challenges.'

~

Arnold Schwarzenegger calls it 'reps'. 'There are no shortcuts,' he says in *Total Recall*, his autobiography. 'It took hundreds and even thousands of repetitions for me to

Intensity of preparation – 'training to win' – conditions the brain and body to perform under pressure. It lets peak performance become automatic. It develops the mindset to win.

learn to hit a great three-quarter back pose, dance the tango in *True Lies*, paint a beautiful birthday card, and say "I'll be back" just the right way . . . No matter what you do in life, it's either reps or mileage.'

And the best kind of practice involves intensity – getting out of your comfort zone, extending yourself. In a phrase heard around the All Blacks' camp, 'If you're not growing anywhere, you're not going anywhere.'

~

'The fight is won or lost,' says Muhammad Ali, 'far away from witnesses – behind the lines, in the gym, and out there on the road, well before I dance under the lights.'

When coaching the Japan speed skating team in the 1990s, Dr Izumi Tabata observed that short, intense training sessions were as effective as longer, more languid sessions in building both anaerobic capacity and VO_2 max, key indicators of fitness. A test

In business, training is often seen as a soft option and is limited to the occasional away-day. However, effective training is intense, regular and repetitious. For world-class results, it should be central to the culture.

group performing short intense bursts of activity increased their anaerobic capacity by 28 per cent and VO_2 max by 15 per cent, compared to a second group training more traditionally, who only improved their VO_2 max by 10 per cent, with no gain in anaerobic capacity.

Meanwhile, the Department of Surgery at Beth Israel Deaconess Medical Center, a teaching hospital in New York City, have developed what they call the 'Top Gun Laparoscopic Skills Shoot-Out', an intensity-based interactive 'video game' for surgeons-in-training. Laparoscopic surgeons who spent three hours a week training on the video game made one third fewer errors and performed 25 per cent faster than those who didn't.

> Training with intensity accelerates personal growth.

~

Intensity training isn't new, of course – military organizations have enjoyed its benefits for millennia; from Spartan regimes in Ancient times to today's dreaded Fartlek Hill, the training course for the US Marine Corps in Quantico, Virginia.

In the eighteenth century Alexander Vasilyevich Suvorov espoused 'constant, progressive and repetitive training under conditions gradually approaching those of genuine combat'. Central to his training programme was an exercise called '*skvoznaia ataka*' ('attack through'). A thousand men would charge from one side, a thousand from the other, at pace and with meaning. Men and horses were injured, some would even die, as the practice was repeated and repeated.

Better to lose a few men in training, Suvorov believed, than lose a battle.

His methods worked. He was never defeated.

In the early 1970s, the US Air Force set up Exercise Red Flag.

Analysts had discovered that after ten successful combat missions the survival rate of pilots improved significantly. The intensity of live combat, it seems, is invaluable training for, well, live combat. Red Flag, based at Nellis Airforce base, Nevada, simulates large-scale, realistic air combat situations. Former Red Arrows pilot Justin Hughes says, 'You're trying to exercise decision-making in high stressed environments. It's role play for real. You'd probably do a week of days – and a week of nights – the bad guys don't sleep at night ... Because we train so hard and so well at it, we tend to be better than everybody else.'

It's not the physical but the psychological aspect that the All Blacks have pioneered – the use of randomness, unpredictability and constant questioning, combined with pace and physicality, in order to stress the brain and test decision-making capacity.

'It's all about performing under pressure on the paddock,' says Gilbert Enoka. And to perform under pressure when it matters, you need to train that way.

That way, when we do it for real, it's automatic. We don't think, we just do.

We have clarity. Accuracy. Intensity.

Train to win.

–

In early 2010, Gilbert Enoka called in the services of Gazing Performance System's Ceri Evans and Renzie Hanham, two men with both a theoretical and a practical understanding of how the brain performs under pressure.

Evans, a karate black belt and former Rhodes Scholar who won fifty-six caps for the New Zealand football team, is a forensic psychiatrist who developed the methodology that Gazing now uses to help organizations lift performance. Hanham has represented his country in karate and coached organizations, as well as sports teams to Olympic level. Gazing works internationally with companies including Xerox, Avis and UPS in handling pressure, improving performance and delivering results.

Evans and Hanham, alongside Henry, Enoka, Smith and Hansen, trainer Nick Gill and the players' Leadership Group, formed the 'Mental Analysis and Development Group' early in 2010 to confront the issue of pressure – what it is, what it does and what they can do about it. They called it MAD for short.

'Just having a knowledge of how the brain reacts to stress was a pretty important first step,' says Henry. 'What the players do, why they felt the way they felt.'

Though unwilling to reveal the specifics of the work Evans and Hanham did with the All Blacks – 'some of it is clinical' – Bede Brosnahan of Gazing was happy to discuss how some of the tools, techniques and methodologies they use with elite teams can apply to the world of business.

'The work we do is all about the control of attention,' says Brosnahan. In pressure situations, he says, it is very easy for our consciousness to 'divert from a resourceful state to an unresourceful one', from a position of mental calm, clarity and inner strength into what he calls 'Defensive Thinking'.

We've all felt it – the sensation as our shutters come down, our horizons narrow and we find ourselves in an ever-tightening corridor from which we feel there is no escape. In this state we're thinking about survival, says Brosnahan. 'A negative content loop' forms and our perceptions create feelings of being overwhelmed, tightening and tension. This in turn leads to unhelpful behaviours – overt aggression, shutting down and panic. We let the situation get to us. We make poor decisions. And we choke.

In Gazing parlance, we are H.O.T.

- Heated
- Overwhelmed
- Tense

They call this 'Red Head'.

The opposite they call 'Blue Head.'

This is the ability to maintain clarity, situational awareness, accurate analysis and good decision-making under pressure. It's a resourceful state in which we are able to trust ourselves to deliver, to be flexible, adaptable and on top of our game. We can see the big picture as well as the important details and our attention is where it should be. To have a Blue Head means to remain on task, rather than diverted, and Gazing's parlance allows us to ACT:

A.	**Alternatives**:	to look at our options, adapt, adjust and overcome
C.	**Consequences**:	to understand the risk/reward ratio of each alternative and to make an accurate assessment of what is needed
T.	**Task Behaviours**:	To stay on task and execute the tactics and strategy

Performance under pressure is knowing how to ACT. In Brosnahan's words, 'allowing yourself to win by following the process rather than being caught up in outcomes'.

'The skill to handle pressure was critical,' says Henry. 'Pressure is a privilege,' says Gilbert Enoka – it means you're playing to the highest level. 'If an organization is really going to be world-class,' Brosnahan elaborates, 'that's going to mean an awful lot of pressure – pressure is a good thing.'

The thing is, he continues, most organizations don't focus on a programme of training for mental toughness. They 'tend to go for the one-off hits, which is unrealistic': a training session, an away day, an inspirational speech, but nothing continuous and progressive. Few focus on long-term development, on a programme of improvement.

'Most people have the will to win,' says basketball coach Bobby Knight, 'few have the will to prepare to win.' Yet, like physical fitness, mental toughness is the result of a long-term conditioning programme.

'It's crazy,' Gilbert Enoka tells *Real Estate Business* magazine, 'because if you want to build up strength, you go to the gym and you work three times a week on your core strength. It just seems that if you want to develop your ability to concentrate and focus and be flexible in what you do from a mental perspective, wouldn't you apply the same approach?'

'If you think of physical conditioning, technical understanding and tactical appreciation as forming three legs,' Wayne Smith tells writer Gregor Paul, 'the stool isn't balanced unless you have psychological strength as well.'

~

Gazing's training approach, in its simplest form, says Brosnahan, involves a 'skill ladder', which begins by building technique and increasing intensity, then introduces real pressure. An everyday example might be in preparation for a speech: first we read through the text, maybe practise in front of the mirror until we've got the words and the flow right;

then we might invite a few people to watch us rehearse – upping the intensity – and then finally, we might introduce real, emotional pressure; a video camera perhaps, a hostile heckler in the room, a bet on the number of times we hesitate, an unrealistic time limit . . .

In this way our brains acclimatize to the pressure. We develop clarity, more accurate, automatic execution and situational awareness.

The idea, however, is not to do too much too soon. A surfeit of pressure applied prematurely will leave us foundering, disoriented and modelling the very emotions we're training to avoid. Just as with cooking a live frog, slowly does it. Let the frog gradually get used to the steadily increasing temperature so that it doesn't jump out.

By the time it realizes 'it's hot in here', it's too late.

So, we focus on the technique, increase the intensity, and then add pressure. Before we finish, we reduce the intensity and focus once again on the technique, as if we're cooling down at the gym. Repeat. And keep repeating until it's automatic.

The technique becomes powerfully embedded and we leave the process with a feeling of control. The point is to give our mental performance what Neuro Linguistic Programming calls 'unconscious competence', and what the All Blacks call 'clarity'.

Henry says, 'When Smithy talks about intensity and accuracy, we're talking about a process of clarity – playing with intensity and accuracy, as opposed to "shit, we've got to win this game. Look at the scoreboard, it's bloody 8-8, we're in the shit here!". And then you freeze and choke, overcompensate, don't trust your mates, all that stuff.'

'It's about striking the balance between being lucid but being motivated,' says Andrew Mehrtens. 'There comes a point where you can become too hyped up and you lose your lucidity and ability to read a situation and make a good decision.'

The word automatic is from the Greek, *Automatus*, and means 'self-thinking'. It's not far from the idea of thinking for yourself – the idea of autonomy and self-responsibility implied by the phrase 'Better People Make Better All Blacks'. By training with intensity, we make our performance more automatic, better able to stay on task. If we can control our attention – avoid the Red and stay in the Blue – we can focus on controlling the things we can control, without worrying about the things we can't.

We can stay in the moment.

We can lead with clarity.

Train to Win

Mastery in anything – a sport, a skill, a craft, business – is achieved by practice. Practice is enhanced by intensity. Research has shown that both our body and our brains respond positively to a diet of accelerated, intense learning, which leads to dramatic improvements and competitive advantage. The All Blacks embrace the power of intensity to 'train to win' – working with randomized scenarios and unexpected challenges in order to recalibrate the players' tolerance for high-pressure situations.

The aim is to enable greater clarity and accuracy under stressful circumstances – and to enhance the ability to bring attention back to the present and the task at hand. Smart leaders utilize intensity to challenge themselves and their teams, and to increase competence and capability. Just as core body exercises are vital for physical conditioning, so core psychological training is essential to develop mental toughness and resilience.

Train to Win

Practise under pressure.

——— *Tangata akona ki te kāinga, tūngia ki te marae,
tau ana.*
A person who is taught at home will stand
with confidence in the community.

IX

PRESSURE

> _Te tīmatanga o te mātauranga ko te wahangū,_
> _te wāhanga tuarua ko te whakarongo._
> The first stage of learning is silence,
> the second stage is listening.

KEEP A BLUE HEAD
Control your attention

New Zealand vs. France, Cardiff, 6 October 2007

The game went the All Blacks' way at first. At half time, the French were trailing 13-3. Then it all went wrong.

By the final whistle Les Bleus had the lead: 20-18.

It was over, the All Blacks defeated in the quarter-final, their World Cup ended.

'The feeling in the sheds was like no-man's land,' Anton Oliver said. 'Sort of desolate, decayed, the smell of – I don't want to dramatize it – but death, you know.'

The pressure had been too much.

The All Blacks had choked.

Again.

'One minute decides the outcome of a battle,' Suvorov wrote, 'one hour the outcome of a campaign, one day the fate of empires.'

The armchair critics said the All Blacks had only to regroup, drive up field and kick for goal. Instead, in the final minutes, they went for the try. It was the wrong option, poor decision-making under pressure, confusion instead of clarity, a lack of leadership.

It cost them the world.

~

'Pressure is expectation, scrutiny and consequence,' says Gilbert Enoka. 'Under pressure, your attention is either diverted or on track. If you're diverted, you have a negative emotional response and unhelpful behaviour. That means you're stuck. That means you're overwhelmed.'

On the other hand, if your attention is on track you have situational awareness and you execute accurately. You are clear, you adapt and you overcome.

~

The All Blacks weren't the first sportsmen to choke, of course.

Greg Norman famously fell apart in the 1986 Masters, relinquishing a six-hole lead going into the final day.

In 1951 the Brooklyn Dodgers were up thirteen games in late August when they allowed the New York Giants to catch up at the end of the season. The Giants famously won the final playoff with a ninth innings three-runner hit by Bobby Thompson.

It was the 'Shot Heard Round the World'.

Meanwhile, the England Football team has won only 17 per cent of their penalty shootouts – compared to Germany's 83 per cent. Football, says former England striker Gary Lineker, is 'a game played for 90 minutes and at the end Germany win.'

Clearly, in any game played with the body, it's the head that counts.

~

'I think most non-elite sportsmen can relate to the fact that, when it is a life changing moment, that's when you're most likely to fluff your lines,' says Matthew Syed, author of *Bounce*, tells Channel 4 News. 'A life defining job interview, you're about to talk to the woman of your dreams . . . and it happened to me. Suddenly I was unable to execute the skills I'd built up over a lifetime.'

Syed was competing at table tennis at the Sydney Olympics when he found he could barely hit the ball. 'Instead of just doing it, using the subconscious part of the brain, which is a very efficient deliverer of a complex task, [people who choke] exert conscious control, and it disrupts the smooth working of the subconscious.'

> Bad decisions are not made through a lack of skill or innate judgement: they are made because of an inability to handle pressure at the pivotal moment.

It's what tennis coach Nick Bollettieri calls the 'centipede effect'. If a centipede had to think about moving all its legs in the right order, it would freeze, the task too complex and daunting. The same is true of humans.

Red is what Suvorov called 'the Dark'. It is that fixated negative content loop of self-judgement, rigidity, aggression, shut down and panic. Blue is what he called 'the Light' – a deep calmness in which you are on task, in the zone, on your game, in control and in flow. It applies to the military; it applies to sport; it applies to business.

RED HEAD
Tight, inhibited, results-oriented, anxious, aggressive, over-compensating, desperate.

BLUE HEAD
Loose, expressive, in the moment, calm, clear, accurate, on task.

In the heat of battle, the difference between the inhibitions of the Red and the freedom of Blue is the manner in which we control our attention.

It works like this: where we direct our mind is where our thoughts will take us; our thoughts create an emotion; the emotion defines our behaviour; our behaviour defines our performance. So, simply, if we can control our attention, and therefore our thoughts, we can manage our emotions and enhance our performance.

Which is easier said than done.

Typical pressure zones are times of great 'heat';

- where something is at stake;
- where trauma of previous experience is triggered;
- where there is conflict, aggression, dispute, dissent;

- where there is a deadline, a ticking clock, urgency;
- where there is high stimulus and distraction.

In these kinds of situations – an impossible deadline at work, for instance, or the final seconds of the knockout stages of a Rugby World Cup – how do we control our attention? How do we stay present? Remain resourceful? Keep on task?

How do we avoid the Red and stay in the Blue?

~

'State changing,' says Wayne Smith, 'is really critical.' Graham Henry saw it as one of the key factors in his team's eventual triumph. 'Having skills to go from red to blue, or maintain the blue, was pretty important in the scheme of things,' he says.

'I think,' says Gilbert Enoka, 'that anyone in our arena who looks at performance and looks at improvement . . . it's all about a state shift . . . and ensuring that you can get your head into a good place.'

For Richie McCaw it's about avoiding what he describes in *The Real McCaw* as 'fight, flight or freeze'. You want to avoid, he says, the 'bad experience pictures from the past or fear of future consequences'. In the language of Neuro-linguistic Programming, his 'preferred representational system' – that is, the way he processes and retains information – is predominantly visual. Throughout *The Real McCaw* he consistently uses visual descriptors to describe his symptoms of stress: 'exercising the strongest will in the world to keep the bad pictures at bay'; 'They're seeing better than me'.

In recognizing his triggers – bad pictures – and controlling his attention – keeping the bad pictures at bay – he is able to stay in the present, remain clear, accurate and on task.

For other people the triggers might be more auditory.

Think of the reaction of an Iraq veteran suffering from post-traumatic stress disorder to a car backfiring. For others it will more kinaesthetic – the feeling of walking into a crowded room; a certain smell such as Marcel Proust's Madeleine cakes. In fact, though we all have our preferred representational system, we also have all the embedded auditory, visual and kinaesthetic triggers. The trick is to recognize when they are firing in our brains and when the effect is negative.

We need to recognize the 'Red Flags', the 'Warning Sirens', our 'Sixth Sense'. Then we have to manage our reactions.

'The brain essentially has three parts – instinct, thinking and emotion,' Enoka told Gregor Paul at The *New Zealand Herald*. 'Invariably under pressure it is the thinking that shuts down and that means you are relying on emotion and instinct and can no longer pick up the cues and information to make good decisions.'

He says, 'If you become disconnected then you can focus on outcome and not task and the ability to make good decisions is compromised.'

The Real McCaw describes the work that Ceri Evans did with the players to help them reconnect. Like meditation, it begins with the breath: 'Breathing slowly and deliberately . . . shift your attention to something external – the ground or your feet, or the ball at hand, or even alternating big toes, or the grandstand . . . use deep breaths and key words to get out of your own head, find an external focus, get yourself "back in the present", regain your situational awareness.'

These actions are Anchors (see Chapter VII), and they have a particular function. They are designed to bring the players into the moment, into clarity, into the blue. It is easy to see how this technique is applicable to a pressurized business environment.

Essentially, it works like this.

First, we put ourself in a resourceful state: calm, positive, clear. Then we 'anchor' that state through a specific, replicable physical action – something out of the ordinary, like scrunching up our toes, stamping our foot, staring into the distance, throwing water over our face. Repeat, and repeat, and repeat – until it's automatic.

Then, when we recognize the symptoms of pressure – when our focus closes down, our vision narrows, our heart rate lifts, our anxiety increases, our self-consciousness rises – we can use the anchor to reboot. And return to our centre. Like a doctor using paddles on a cardiac arrest, the 'jolt of recognition' reactivates our more resourceful state and returns us to the moment.

It is, literally, 're-cognition': thinking again. Undiverted, we're free to assess, adjust and act; to become realigned with our task and the best way to complete it.

To act rather than react.

~

'What do pilots do when they're crashing?' Gazing's Bede Brosnahan asks before answering his own question. 'They look at the manual.'

He's joking, he says, but it is a good way to anchor the Gazing Performance System's methodology. Gazing, he explains, develop 'maps' for their clients – simple schematics that clarify the issues and provide an easily recalled point of reference in pressure situations.

'Maps force clarity,' he says. 'You can't put bullshit on a map.'

In high-performing domains, he says, people have the same maps, the same common language. This common language – whether a schematic, words, phrases or mantras – delivers clarity. 'If you have a direction you want to go in, if you can describe it, succinctly and clearly, that's your starting point,' he says.

The map is not the terrain – but it sure helps when you get a little lost.

> Mantras are the way in which we can tell our story to ourselves; they are tools for effective thinking, a mental roadmap in times of pressure.

And maps exist on many levels – visual mnemonics of the sort that Gazing uses, physical triggers of the kind that McCaw explains, and words or mantras designed to bring you into the moment.

'I can still remember them,' says Anton Oliver, recalling the playing mantra the All Blacks used in his day. 'TQB, top-quality ball. OTG, over the gain line. KBA, keep the ball alive. And LQB, lightening quick ball. You get these four things going, we're fine … That gave us the template to figure out the game.'

Originally, the mantra was a word, phrase or sound with the power to transform. Vedic in origin, the most famous example is 'Om' – the meditative mantra that brings the adept into the moment. Its purpose hasn't changed: mantras are literally an 'instrument for thinking', a practical tool for returning to the moment.

Pilots, for instance, have a mantra to help them deal with a deluge of flight data that assails them during a crisis:

_____ Aviate.

Navigate.

Communicate.

That is, first focus on flying the plane; second, fly the plane in the right direction; third, tell people where you're flying the plane. It's a simple, practical process that has saved lives. Its simplicity enables pilots to orient themselves and take the right steps in the right order; providing big-picture perspective and clearly defined steps.

Meanwhile, paramedics and ski patrollers have a mantra for first-aid situations.

_____ Assess.

Adjust.

Act.

That is, assess the situation; adjust your approach to suit the situation; act accordingly. Again, the process creates clarity and certainty, without losing urgency.

The thing many mantras share is the Rule of Three; that is, they are three words or phrases that work together in a stepwise process to bring about change.

The Rule of Three is the way humans tell stories; with a beginning, a middle and an end. You'll see it in drama with the three-act play, in jokes with 'an Englishman, an Irishman and a Scotsman', and in an orator's rhetoric: Adolf Hitler's '*Ein Volk, ein Reich, ein Führer*', for instance, or the desire for 'life, liberty and the pursuit of happiness', or the Māori proverb, *Titiro, whakarongo, kōrero* (Look, listen, then speak).

By harnessing this three-point structure, mantras create a strong linguistic chain of events; they take you from chaos, through clarity and into action.

Automatically.

~

Controlling our attention – through anchoring, maps and mantras – is about bringing ourselves back into the present.

Rather than 'what ifs', we are then able to deal with the 'what is'.

Rather than, 'What if we run out of resources?' we can ask, 'What is the best way to use our resources?'

Rather than, 'What if I don't win the contract?' we can ask, 'What can I do to win the contract?'

Maps and mantras allows us to, in Gilbert Enoka's phrase, 'meet pressure with pressure'; that is, rather than feeling it, we can apply it. By controlling our attention we control our performance, by controlling our performance we control the game.

So, fast forward from Cardiff 2007 to Auckland 2011, from a Rugby World Cup quarter-final to a World Cup final, from a team heading towards defeat to a team heading towards victory.

It's the same two sides playing: New Zealand vs. France. It's just as tight, but this time New Zealand lead by one point.

Read the body language.

Richie McCaw breathes, holds his wrist, stamps his feet – reconnecting with himself, returning to the moment.

He looks around. There are no glazed eyes now. No walking dead.

Brad Thorne throws water over himself, cooling his thoughts. Kieran Read stares out to the far distant edge of the stadium, regaining perspective.

New Zealand, the stadium of four million people, is less calm. The dread casts a long black cloud. The spectators can't help but flash back to the bad pictures. They are in the Red, but the All Blacks stay in the Blue.

The clock counts itself down, slowly, slowly; until finally . . . the whistle blows.

8–7 New Zealand.

'We smashed 'em,' says Graham Henry.

And in their heads, they did.

Keep a Blue Head

Pressure is 'expectation, scrutiny and consequence'. It is the curtain coming down, the shutters closing, the red mist rising. It leads to tightening, panic, over-aggression, choking – and poor decision-making under pressure. Wise leaders seek to understand how the brain reacts to stress and practise simple, almost meditative techniques to stay calm, clear and connected. They use maps, mantras and anchors to navigate their way through highly pressurized situations, both personal and professional, and to bring themselves back to the moment. In this way they and their teams stay on top of their game and on top of the situation. These techniques can take us from a volatile, uncertain and ambiguous space into a place of mental clarity. 'Clear thought. Clear talk. Clear task.' They are the difference between Red and Blue, dark and light, failure and success.

Keep a Blue Head

Control your attention.

—— *Mā te rongo, ka mōhio;*
Mā te mōhio, ka mārama;
Mā te mārama, ka mātau;
Mā te mātau, ka ora.

From listening comes knowledge;
From knowledge comes understanding;
From understanding comes wisdom;
From wisdom comes well-being.

X

AUTHENTICITY

—— *Whakapūpūtia mai ō mānuka, kia kore ai e whati.*
Cluster the branches of the manuka, so that they
will not break.

KNOW THYSELF
  Keep it real

'We always talk about the "real self" rather than the "fake self",' says Gilbert Enoka. 'If you come into the All Blacks and you succumb to peer pressure, and you do things because others want you to, if you're not grounded then . . . you get found out.'

Enoka uses the analogy of a bridge that is secure because it is made of several different planks: personal skills, friends, family, being an All Black. 'If the only plank you've got is the rugby one, then you'll always come unstuck.'

He explains how the All Blacks learn to protect themselves from mental fragility. 'If you marry the self, the environment, the culture, the rituals, the legacy, and you put these together, you actually weave a pretty powerful fabric that'll actually get you through your journey. You may wobble a bit (when things go wrong), but you won't actually fracture and crumble.'

Better People Make Better All Blacks.

~

Know thyself.

Often attributed to Socrates, the phrase is even older, inscribed in the Inner Chamber of Luxor Temple, in Upper Egypt.

'Man, know thyself,' the hieroglyphs say, 'and thou shalt know the Gods.'

'To know how to win,' goes the saying, 'you first have to know how to lose.' For the All Blacks, to know how to lose, you first have to know who you are.

In refusing to be distracted by the clamour of the crowds, the distractions of the day, we can become free to follow our own path; to, in Enoka's words, 'be resilient and to stand tall and to keep faith and stay strong within yourself'.

'Development of the authentic self,' he says, 'is hugely powerful to performance.'

It is the essence of the leader, his base, his *mana*.

In his landmark book, *True North*, Harvard Business School professor Bill George argues that the essence of a great leader is about 'being genuine, real and true to who you are'. It's an approach reflected within the All Blacks' camp.

Enoka says of McCaw, 'people say to him, how do you manage the public arena? And he said, "Well, it's easy, because what you see in public is exactly what I'm like in private."'

'Most leaders who fail,' Bill George says in an interview with Pamela Hawley, 'really suffer from a lack of a strong identity, belief in themselves and, to be frank, respect for themselves. When leaders are disrespecting others, it really starts with themselves.'

> The best leaders remain true to their deepest values. They lead their own life and others follow.

'First we do need to take a look at the meaning behind life,' he says. 'Leaders need to think: "Why are you here? What's your purpose? How do I use my time here?"'

It is reminiscent of Buckminster Fuller:

'What is my job on the planet? What is it that needs doing, that I know something about, that probably won't happen unless I take responsibility for it?'

'I believe that leadership begins and ends with authenticity,' says George. 'It's being yourself, being the person you were created to be.' Adopting the styles of other leaders is the opposite of authenticity.

'Your time is limited,' Steve Jobs said in his now famous 2005 Stanford Commencement address, 'don't be trapped by dogma . . . And most important, have the courage to follow your heart and intuition. They somehow already know what you truly want to become. Everything else is secondary.'

Authenticity is the opposite of Jean-Paul Sartre's *mauvaise foi*, or bad faith.

Bad faith occurs when peer pressure and social forces combine to have us disown our own values. It is an accommodation we make with society to fit in, a psychological 'selling out' in which we forsake our own freedom and self-expression for the conformity of the crowd. Worse, it stands between our self and ourselves. It stops us knowing our true nature, which cauterizes our *mana*.

In *Essays in Existentialism*, Sartre uses the example of the waiter whose style has become mannered, 'quick and forward, a little too rapid'. This distance between self and self-projection, reality and identity betrays him, removes him from his true purpose, and alienates those around him.

On the other hand, authenticity allows us to *author* our own lives; to make our own original imprint and to write our own story in a voice that is true to our values.

'I want to live an authentic life,' says Anton Oliver. 'But of course to do that you have to understand who you are first. To have a baseline to keep referring back to.'

And this begins with honesty and integrity.

First, Honesty

'In the belly, not the back' is how Gilbert Enoka describes it – the ability to deliver honest feedback. Owen Eastwood considers it a prerequisite of a peak performing environment:

_____ *The key to strong peer-to-peer interaction is a high level of trust. This is trust in the sense of safe vulnerability. The leaders need to create an environment where individuals get to know each other as people and gather insight into their*

*personal story and working style. This needs to be supported
by the leader's role-modelling behaviour around admission
of mistakes and weaknesses and fears ... This is essential
for safe conflict and safe confrontation, where the most
important interaction often occurs.*

'I think early on we didn't deal with losing very well,' says
Anton Oliver. 'It was very much point the finger, everyone very
isolated. That changed a lot as the team became more collective,
took the burden of loss equally, shared it.'

'I enjoy watching the game together as a team because
everything's out in the open,' says Andrew Mehrtens. 'Your missed
tackles are out in the open, things you have done well are out in the
open ... Being able to say to another guy and just being matter of fact without it being a personal
judgement, "You need to be doing this to help me out with my
job." Or, equally, "What can I do that helps you do your job?"'

> **High-performing teams
> promote a culture
> of honesty, authenticity
> and safe conflict.**

If you are able to do that, Mehrtens says, 'I think you've got
a good team.'

And Then, Integrity

Integrity comes from the Latin *integritas* or integer. It means
being whole and undivided. It is the ethical 'accuracy of
our actions'.

Integrity means that our thoughts and words and deeds
are 'as one', a chiropractic alignment in which our core values,
purpose, beliefs and behaviours all flow in the same direction.
It's useful to think of integrity not as morality, as many people
do, but as *workability*. It is not about being pure, or noble – it's

about getting stuff done. Though the end result is trust, belief and respect, these are merely the by-products of the fact that when we say something will happen, it actually does happen.

This means that others can count on us to deliver. And, most importantly, that we can count on ourselves.

~

In a paper published at Harvard Business School, Michael C. Jensen, Werner Erhard and Steve Zaffron explore the relationship between integrity and performance. In the abstract for their model – 'Integrity: Where Leadership Begins' – they define their terms:

_____ *Integrity in our model is honoring your word. As such, integrity is a purely positive phenomenon. It has nothing to do with good vs. bad, right vs. wrong behavior. Like the law of gravity, the law of integrity just is, and if you violate the law of integrity ... you get hurt just as if you try to violate the law of gravity with no safety device. The personal and organizational benefits of honoring one's word are huge – both for individuals and for organizations – and generally unappreciated.*

It is a simple and powerful concept. Integrity is, they say, 'a factor of production as important as knowledge or technology' that 'provides access to incredible increases in performance'.

Think of the time wasted at meetings in which people are late or don't turn up, deadlines that drift, phone calls never made because 'something came up', cheques in the mail, relationships ruined because one side let the other side down. Systems failing to mesh, to adhere, to work together properly.

But what if they did? What if everything worked like clockwork, together, predictably and on time?

Jansen *et al.* posit what they call the Ontological Law of Integrity:

_____ *To the degree that integrity is diminished, the opportunity for performance is diminished.*

That is, the more slippage there is, the less gets done; and the less slippage, the more traction. They compare it to a bicycle wheel. If spokes are missing, the wheel works less efficiently. If all the spokes are in place, it's as efficient as it can possibly be. Integrity means all the spokes are in place, all the time.

Unsurprisingly, there is a rigorous integrity within the All Blacks camp, an almost total accountability. 'When deeds speak,' says Wayne Smith, 'words are nothing.' If someone says they'll do something, you can be sure they will do it. If they say they'll be somewhere, they will be there. In fact, they work to Lombardi's rule: if you're not early for a meeting, you're late. Many set their watches ten minutes fast. No one is late for the bus. No one wants to let anyone down.

It gets the job done.

> If integrity is a central leadership tool and everyone in a team does exactly what they say they will do, clarity, certainty, productivity and momentum are the results.

~

If we have a compelling purpose, high expectations and clear goals, but we don't honour them, we get nowhere. But by focusing on this specific area – on 'accuracy of action' – we can change the relationship we have with our own thoughts, and this is tremendously powerful. Rather than vague ideas and intentions, if we are our word to ourselves, then our thoughts become more committed, intentional and decisive.

They become agents of change.

'Authenticity,' according to leadership writer Lance Secretan, 'is the alignment of head, mouth, heart and feet – thinking, saying and doing the same thing consistently. This builds trust, and followers love leaders they can trust.'

Honesty = Integrity = Authenticity = Resilience = Performance

If leaders make their word a commitment – 'I am going to make this happen' – tremendous things begin to occur and businesses, empires, fortunes and legacies are built. If the conversation we have with ourselves has integrity, then the results can be revolutionary.

There's a old story about J. P. Morgan, the banker and philanthropist, who was shown an envelope containing a 'guaranteed formula for success'. He agreed that if he liked the advice written inside he would pay $25,000 for its contents.

Morgan opened the envelope, nodded, and paid.

The advice?

1. Every morning write a list of the things that need to be done that day.

2. Do them.

~

By being aware of integrity slippage, we can cultivate discipline, intention and action, both personally and within our teams.

If we speak with integrity our word becomes our world; a commitment, a declaration of intent, a generative force. It allows us to speak with optimism and possibility, resilience and determination, decisiveness and authority. It helps us survive any setback. And it helps us begin the long climb back upwards again.

With an authentic voice, we have authority.

We can author our own story.

Know Thyself

In recognizing our deepest values, we can understand what kind of leader we are and what kind of life we wish to lead. Authenticity – the mark of a true leader – begins with honesty and integrity. Honesty allows us access to our truest vision of ourselves and, when setbacks occur, gives us strong foundations. Integrity gets the job done. If our values, thoughts, words and actions are aligned, then our word is our world. With accuracy of action, less slippage occurs between thought and deed. In knowing ourselves, we live our vision. By being our word, we make it happen.

Know Thyself

Keep it real.

_____ *He tangata kī tahi.*

A person who can be taken at his word.

XI

SACRIFICE

—— *Ka tū te ihiihi.*
Stand fearless.

CHAMPIONS DO EXTRA
Find something you
would die for and give
your life to it

'I was in the hotel,' says Benson Stanley, a young man about to make his All Blacks debut, 'when one of the senior guys comes up to me, tapped me on the shoulder and gave me two questions to think about ... First, what do I have to offer the team? ... And, second, what am I prepared to sacrifice?' He pauses. 'Pretty big questions.'

That night Stanley and a number of other rookies were called in front of the team. They answered the questions. What can I offer? What will I sacrifice? Then a few of the senior players – Richie McCaw, Conrad Smith, Brad Thorn – spoke about what it means to be an All Black, the legacy, the standards, the players who have laid their bodies on the line before them. Then the whole team performed a *haka* to welcome the new recruits, and to challenge them.

'From then on I knew it was the big time,' says Stanley. That's when he knew he was an All Black.

~

Initiation ceremonies 'ease the transition from one state into another,' writes Joseph Campbell in *Myths to Live By*. From youth to maturity, freedom to responsibility, life into death, they are a psychological passageway. A process of becoming.

'A ritual is an enactment of a myth,' Campbell says. 'By participating in a ritual, you are participating in a myth.' A primary All Blacks myth is the idea of sacrifice. Giving everything for the team, bleeding for it, putting your balls on the line.

Giving everything you have.

And a little bit more.

~

'Champions do extra.' It's Brad Thorn talking now.

The opposite of a rookie, Thorn played more than 200 Rugby League games for the Brisbane Broncos before switching codes and playing sixty Tests for the All Blacks, becoming a World Cup final winner. In honours won – and respect earned – he is one of the most successful rugby players of all time. As he talks, younger All Blacks strain to hear what he has to say.

He was a lazy kid, he says, but his father had a motto that he now uses every day:

_____ *Champions do extra.'*

First to arrive at the gym, and the last to leave, Thorn's motto means he always adds something extra to the end of every routine – an extra rep, an extra ten minutes, an extra set, an extra circuit. 'Five minutes to go in the Test match,' he asks, 'who wants it more?'

~

There is a saying: 'There are no crowds lining the extra mile.' On the extra mile, we are on our own: just us and the road, just us and the blank sheet of paper, just us and the challenge we've set ourself. It's the work we do behind closed doors that makes the difference out on the field of play, in whichever field we compete, whether we're in a team, leading a business or just leading our life.

Much has been written about the agony of the long-distance runner, the loneliness of the artist in their garret, and the kinds of sacrifice – of time, comfort, socializing, hedonism – that it takes to make the transition from ordinary to extraordinary, good to great, but the winning difference is most neatly encapsulated in the mantra given to Thorn by his father.

Champions do extra.

Another father; another gift to a promising son . . .

Neville Carter wanted to give his son Daniel something

special for his eighth birthday, so waiting on the back lawn one morning was a set of full-size rugby posts, painted in the blue and white of Southbridge, the local rugby club.

'He'd be out there for hours and hours,' Neville told the *New Zealand Herald*. 'Every day after school and in the weekends.' He would even kick the ball over the house, breaking drainpipes, his father says, but never a window.

Dan Carter became the highest points scorer in Test history.

Champions do extra.

Around the age of thirteen, brothers Ben and Owen Franks told their father, Ken, that they wanted to be All Blacks. Pretty much every New Zealand boy tells his father this at some point but Ken, a personal trainer, took them seriously. 'It wasn't a pushy parent thing,' he says, 'you have to have that drive, and they did. So first we set some goals . . . where you want to be in one year, in five years, but also where you want to be in six months, one month, one week, tomorrow.'

He says, 'We got them into the gym – just technical stuff, you know, building the platform. But by the time they were eighteen they were lifting more than the All Blacks of that time.' The brothers now prop the All Blacks scrum. 'Everything they do is at intensity . . . It's the business of Ben and Owen – it's something they invest in. You don't rest on your laurels; you're always seeking that perfection.'

Within a couple of weeks of winning the World Cup Ben flew in a trainer from the States. 'These are the things I need to work on,' Ben told him, 'these are my weaknesses.'

Champions do extra.

In 1986, the story goes, Buck Shelford was leading his men against France in a Test match now known as 'The Battle of Nantes'. It was brutal. And it was bloody. Early in the game, a French boot raked and ripped Shelford's scrotum. They say a testicle was showing. He limped to the sideline, where a medic stitched up his scrotum, without anaesthetic, before he returned to the field and kept on playing. Shelford later came off, not because of the testicular injury, but because he was concussed, with two teeth missing.

It's a particularly All Blacks brand of courage this – to never surrender, to spill blood for the team, to sacrifice.

To put your balls on the line.

Champions do extra.

It's true in all kinds of sport. There's the story of marksman Károly Takács who was denied a place in the 1936 Olympics as, in pre-war Hungary, only officers could qualify. Undeterred, he set his sights on the 1940 games. But in 1938 a hand grenade shattered his right hand, his shooting hand. He trained himself to shoot with his left hand but the 1940 and 1944 Olympics were cancelled as war ravaged Europe. Finally, in 1948, thirty-eight-year-old Takács competed in his first Olympic event, winning gold and setting a new world record, a right-hander shooting left-handed.

Champions do extra.

It doesn't just apply to sport. As a young *Time* journalist, writer Hunter S. Thompson copied out the entire texts of Scott Fitzgerald's *The Great Gatsby* and Hemingway's *Farewell to Arms*, twice. As his friend Johnny Depp told the *Guardian*, 'He wanted to know what it felt like to write a masterpiece.' Thompson went on to invent Gonzo, a genre that combines the objectivity of journalism with the subjectivity of the novelist. He has been called the greatest American comic writer of the twentieth century.

Champions do extra.

According to Walter Isaacson in *Steve Jobs*, the Apple

founder rejected the circuit board of the Apple II because 'the lines are too close together'. He insisted on reducing the start-up time on early Macs by ten seconds calculating that, with five million users, this would save over 'a hundred lifetimes a year'. Later, when Jobs built a factory in California, he had the floors painted white in search of purity and perfection. 'I want it to be as beautiful as possible,' he said, 'even if it's inside the box. A great carpenter isn't going to use lousy wood for the back of a cabinet, even though nobody's going to see it.'

At the time of Jobs's death, Apple was the most valuable company in the world.

Champions do extra.

'What does self-sacrifice mean to you?' It's a question Andrew Mehrtens asks the teams he coaches. 'It's everything in a team ... Pushing yourself outside your comfort zone ... It's doing extra, doing extra from what you're asked to do, or doing extra from what someone else will do. "Train harder than a non-All Black," we used to say.'

'What's the most important thing in life to you?' asks Sean Fitzpatrick. 'If you ask most business people that, or most sportsmen, they'll say family's number one, work's number two, but then if you actually sit down and think, "Well actually, no Work's actually number one, family's number two", and then you might think to yourself, "You bloody horrible person, that's terrible", but if you want to be the best in the world, you've got to put that at number one ... you've got to make huge sacrifices.'

~

A story.

Once described as 'the most famous man in the British Empire', Dave Gallaher led the 1905 Originals and is considered 'the father of All Blacks rugby'. His team had a brilliant, irrepressible style, playing twenty-five games, losing only one in controversial circumstances when, it is still maintained, the Welsh players dragged Bob Deans, the try-scorer, back from the line before the exhausted referee could catch up. This exceptional team scored 747 points, and only conceded 53. They began the All Blacks legacy.

At irregular intervals, en route to the autumn internationals in Europe, today's All Blacks stop over at a small cemetery in France in order to pay tribute. In Nine Elms British Cemetery, near Ypres, Grave No. 32513 is marked with the silver fern and the name Dave Gallaher, who was struck by shrapnel in the attack on Gravenstafel Spur on 4 October 1917 and died later that day. He was forty-three.

War makes few distinctions between men. As the Italian proverb says, 'At the end of the game, the king and the pawn go back in the same box'.

'It's not letting you get too much up yourself,' says Andrew Mehrtens of the pilgrimage. 'You are part of something far bigger. And at the end of the day when you are playing rugby and you are feeling like you are asked to make certain sacrifices, it's good to remember there are a lot of people who have made far greater sacrifices.'

Whatever we give our life to – whether a business or a project, a family or a sport, a cause or an art or a belief – we are always making sacrifices. Whether we are giving up an hour, or a day, or a lifetime, we are *spending our lives*.

We are *giving our lives for it*.

Every day we go to work, every meeting that bores us, everything we do just for money or out of obligation, all the time we kill, we are giving our life for it. So it better be worthwhile.

Pyschology professor Steven Pinker wrote, 'Wisdom consists of appreciating the preciousness and finiteness of our own existence, and therefore not squandering it.'

'We don't get a chance to do that many things,' said Steve Jobs, 'and every one should be really excellent. Because this is our life. Life is brief, and then you die, you know? And we've all chosen to do this with our lives. So it better be damn good. It better be worth it.'

Stephen Covey encouraged us to begin at the end, imagining ourselves at our own funeral. Who would be there? What would they say about us once we're gone? What would our life mean to them? Would they cry?

This isn't morbid, but the opposite. It means putting something at stake – our life. It means a sense of urgency and immediacy, and it is good to have a bit of urgency and immediacy in life.

If we're going to *lead* a life, if we're going to lead anything, we should surely know where we are going, and why.

Champions do extra.

They find something that they are prepared to die for.

Then they give their life to it.

Champions Do Extra

The motto 'Champions do extra' refers to the extra, discretionary effort and sacrifice it takes to do something extraordinary. Whatever we do in life, we're giving our life for it, so we best be sure it is worth it. Killing time is slow suicide. Treading water is drowning. So, what are we prepared to give our life to? As leaders, what kind of life will we lead? It begins by doing extra; the extra set at the gym, the extra burst of hard work, the extra sprint, the extra effort. Think of Buckminster Fuller: 'What is my job on the planet? What is it that needs doing, that I know something about, that probably won't happen unless I take responsibility for it?' What is the extra that will make us extraordinary?

Champions Do Extra

Find something you would die for and give your life to it.

———— *Kaua e mate wheke, mate ururoa.*

Don't die like an octopus, die like a hammerhead shark.

XII

LANGUAGE

——— *Taringa whakarongo.*
Let your ears listen.

INVENT YOUR
OWN LANGUAGE
Sing your world
into existence

In 1999, John Kirwan and Sean Fitzpatrick decided to write a book.

Standards were slipping. So were results – the All Blacks had lost five games in a row. The recently retired pair felt that no one was passing the principles on, so they decided to do something about it.

It became known as 'The Black Book', and was for All Blacks' eyes only, on pain of excommunication, almost. For a time it became the team bible and its collected wisdom, in the form of aphorisms, still informs the culture.

- No one is bigger than the team.
- Leave the jersey in a better place.
- Live for the jersey. Die for the jersey.
- It's not enough to be a good. It's about being great.
- Leave it all out on the field.
- It's not the jersey. It's the man in the jersey.
- Once an All Black, always an All Black.
- Work harder than an ex-All Black.
- In the belly – not the back.
- It's an honor, not a job.
- Bleed for the jersey.
- Front up – or fuck off.

The Black Book was, writes Fitzpatrick in *Winning Matters*, 'a system of meanings that everyone understood – a language and vocabulary and a set of beliefs that bound the group together.'

Not everyone was convinced it was needed. 'In my day you didn't have to write this bloody stuff down,' said one old warhorse. Never the most literate of cultures, the All Blacks' belief system – it's ethos – had been handed down from player to player, team to team, generation to generation, by word of mouth and by example; meaning, rituals, stories, heroes, all bound together by a common, sacred language.

An oral culture.

A common story.

~

Daniel Kahneman writes in *Thinking, Fast and Slow* about the power of our stories to change and shape our lives, often in ways of which we are not aware. Remember, stories don't need to be true to be real. Kahneman tells the story of when he pulled up beside a bus the day after a terrorist attack on another bus – his rational mind knew that the chance of it happening again was low, almost non-existent, yet his emotional brain presented another story and wanted to get the hell away from there. Or there is the story that we tell ourselves as we buy a lottery ticket: we know we have almost no possible chance of winning, yet we still imagine what will happen when we do. The truth never gets in the way of a good story.

> Leaders are storytellers. All great organizations are born from a compelling story. This central organizing thought helps people understand what they stand for and why.

True or not, stories are the way we understand life and our place in it. We are 'meaning making machines', interpreting and reinterpreting a sequence of events into a narrative form and reassembling at will.

As children, stories teach us the difference between right and wrong, good and bad, loyalty and love – our ideas of the way life is, should be and could be. Once we're adults – as advertisers, filmmakers, novelists, journalists and politicians all know –

stories help us understand who we are, what we want, what we stand for, what we stand against, and why we do things.

As in the *The Songlines*, the stories we tell through language still sing our world into existence.

In *Man's Search for Meaning*, Victor Frankl says, 'the striving to find meaning is the primary motivational force in man' – and stories are the way we construct and find meaning in our lives. We should not, he says, 'be hesitant about challenging man with a potential meaning for him to fulfill'. 'One should not search for an abstract meaning of life,' he says. 'Everyone has his own specific vocation or mission in life to carry out, a concrete assignment which demands fulfillment.'

As leaders, it is our job to set that 'concrete assignment'. Whether it is to be 'the best team that has ever played', or a G. A. B. or putting a dent in the universe, it is expressed in language, and imagined as a future memory.

As Kevin Roberts says, 'Revolutions start with language.' Key to effective leadership in the All Blacks' model is how we tell that story, using language to help our people 'connect to the core', using values, vocabulary, mottos, mantras and metaphor.

Values

'Humility, honesty, integrity, respect,' says Sean Fitzpatrick, 'you know, I say all those words and for me and for the people I'm speaking to I'm saying, "Look, you shouldn't really need to work on those because they should just be a given."'

'Values,' writes Frankl, 'cannot be espoused and adopted by us at a conscious level – they are something that we are.' Which is not to say that they cannot be worked on and defined – and captured into a living document that makes a difference.

At the same time as Fitzpatrick and Kirwan were asking

ex-All Blacks what it all meant, Saatchi & Saatchi were working with the NZRU to define the team's brand values. This long consultative process revealed a group of words, which included New Zealand, Winning, Power, Masculinity, Commitment, Teamwork, Tradition and Inspirational – as well as three words that would become core to the All Blacks:

- Humility
- Excellence
- Respect

Sacred values are, of course, the bulwarks that have sustained some of the world's most successful organizations. Faith, Hope and Charity, for instance, or, at the other end of the scale, those of the United States Marine Corps:

_____ *Honour*
Integrity, Responsibility, Accountability.

_____ *Courage*
Do the right thing, in the right way, for the right reason.

_____ *Commitment*
Devotion to the Corps and my fellow Marines.

The Marines' core values are handed out to every recruit on a red card they are expected to carry with them at all times. 'I have them tattooed on my heart,' says one Marine.

'As Marines, we're held to a higher standard,' says another.

After all, if you're going to die for something, it helps to know what you're dying for.

Perhaps the new archetype of the values-based, purpose-driven company is Apple. In the early days of the company (as Walter Isaacson writes in his book, *Steve Jobs*), Mike Markkula wrote the 'Apple Marketing Philosophy', a document which sought to define the company's values.

> Companies that maintain their core values are those that stand alone, stand apart and stand for something.

_____ *Empathy*
We will truly understand [customer] needs better than any other company.

_____ *Focus*
In order to do a good job of those things that we decide to do, we must eliminate all of the unimportant opportunities.

_____ *Impute*
People DO judge a book by its cover. We may have the best products, the highest quality, the most useful software, etc; if we present them in a slipshod manner, they will be perceived as slipshod; if we present them in a creative, professional manner, we will impute the desired properties.

Anyone who has ever opened a piece of Apple packaging, experienced an Apple interface, coveted an Apple product or bought Apple shares will know how powerful these values are.

Meanwhile humility is not the first word that you would imagine belonging to a team of ruthless world champions, yet, alongside excellence and respect, it is central to the All Blacks' core values.

The idea of humility as a central value grounds the team, creates respect, encourages curiosity and generates bonds that sustain them in the heat of battle.

It is a deceptively tough word that is communicated in everything they do: it's part of their story. 'Once you have determined what your set of behaviours are,' says Wayne Smith, 'and what you are striving to achieve, you have to keep feeding it.'

Leaders have to develop concrete actions so that values become part of the story. In the All Blacks, it's about the sweeping of sheds, the signing of autographs, the Rugby Club, the charity work, the connections with the community, the hospital visits, the simple stuff. The being of team.

> Words start revolutions.

Successful cultures are organic and adaptive, they change and flow, yet always just under the surface is a bedrock of values, smoothed by the current above, but unyielding.

'The success was being really good at that,' says Smith, 'really good at making our team talks, our reviews, or game plans, all apply to the central story.'

First we shape our values; then our values shape us.

Vocabulary

In Chapter VII, we looked at the Florida Effect – the way that priming works and the effect that the language around us unconsciously affects our experience of the world. Advertising agencies know this, of course – the word 'new' in a brochure has the power to increase readership. 'For a limited time only' can create almost unlimited enquiries.

Within the All Blacks, as within other high-performing

environments like the Marines, the Red Arrows and Apple, there is a similar obsession with the formative power of language.

- 'Outstanding'
- 'Accuracy'
- 'Clarity'
- 'World class'
- 'Red hot, we were red hot today'

When Wayne Smith joined the Chiefs after the All Blacks, he helped mastermind a linguistic revolution in the team. 'We started establishing a vocabulary, a mindset and an attitude,' he says, and *Māoritanga* – Māori culture – became part of the common language. Attack became *paoa*, meaning 'to strike', and defence became *tainui*, or 'surging tide'.

The pre-season activity retraced the steps of local Māori tribes as they settled in the North Island – a tough, physical journey. This vivid, metaphorical language became the beginning of a rugby revolution.

Words start revolutions.

Mottos and Mantras

As we see in the Black Book, mottos and mantras are a key part of the road-map to the All Blacks' mindset. These linguistic heuristics go straight to the heart of the belief system, becoming shorthand for the standards and behaviour that is expected. Likewise, the spirit of Apple is captured in the language around the Cupertino campus in California:

- Stay Hungry. Stay Foolish.
- Why Join the Navy when you can be a Pirate?

- Insanely Great
- Think Different
- 'Click. Boom. Amazing!'

Even the address of the corporate headquarters is infused with the Apple spirit:

——— *One Infinite Loop.*

Similarly, the spirit of the Marines is captured in their mottos and mantras:

- Once a Marine Always a Marine
- Ductus Exemplo – Lead by Example
- Doing the Right Thing
- Held to a Higher Standard
- First to Fight
- Whatever the Nation Asks
- Semper Fidelis – Always Faithful

Common to all these elite teams and organizations is the use of smart, sharp, easily recognized and understood code-phrases to define and declare their essential spirit. This is not empty sloganeering – when done properly, this kind of compressed thinking in a sentence is one of the leader's most powerful tools. It aligns companies, countries and cultures behind their distilled essence.

Think about the best corporate slogans:

- Just Do It
- Nothing is Impossible

- ° Impossible is Nothing
- ° The Power of Dreams
- ° Think
- ° Invent

They capture character in a sentence, change minds with a turn of phrase, and distil essence into a few words. The best teams – the All Blacks, Apple, the Marines, Nike, Honda, Adidas – harness the power of these mottos and mantras to reflect, remind, reinforce and reinvigorate their ethos, every day.

The wise leader would do well to follow.

Words start revolutions.

Metaphors

The word metaphor comes from the Greek *metaphora*. *Meta* means 'over or across' and *Pherein* means to carry. A metaphor is a figure of speech in which a word or phrase is overlaid on to something to which it is not literally applicable – in which an idea carries over and transforms meaning.

Metaphors are a powerful and often unappreciated leadership tool. Some would argue that they are the basis for our understanding of life itself. In fact, if we believe Friedrich Nietzsche, all language is a metaphor – 'What strange simplification and falsification mankind lives on!' For him, words and language are separate from the thing they describe, an analogy of reality, a simulacrum. 'We possess nothing but metaphors for things,' he writes, 'metaphors which correspond in no way to the original entities.' Though there may well be metaphysics – a substance to reality – in *his* worldview, we are unable to process and understand it, so we take a stab through language, metaphor and story.

Metaphors are where we recognize ourselves in stories – a way we attach personal meaning to a more public narrative. They create a visceral response, and force us to rethink meaning.

We, literally, *re-cognize*.

This metaphorical nature of mind is essential to understand what drives human action. 'It is precisely through metaphor that our perspectives, or analogical extensions, are made,' says American literary theorist Kenneth Burke. 'A world without metaphor would be a world without purpose.'

'The greatest thing by far,' said Aristotle in *Poetics*, 'is to have a command of metaphor. This alone cannot be imparted by another; it is the mark of genius, for to make good metaphors implies an eye for resemblance.'

So then, a story.

One November evening in London, Wayne Smith was attending the theatre, his mind ticking over. When the show finished, he hurried back to his hotel and wrote something down.

The Story of the Black Plague

'I thought . . . I must get the numbers off the jersey and place them on a black background – and it looked like a plague smothering England and I thought it was a magnificent thing to see . . . I decided to name this the Black Plague.'

The Black Plague became the nickname for – and the distillation of – the All Blacks' defensive attitude and approach. 'The boys understood the irony of it and the power of it as well,' says Smith, 'how the Black Plague hit Europe and there were so many victims . . .'

_____ *The Black Plague started in Asia last year then it*

devastated Europe ... destroying everything in its path
... the small, the sick, the slow and the fast.
... It was 366 minutes of tryless tests
... the disease that has devastated Europe is
re-emerging worldwide
... what will it look like?
... fast, pressure through set pieces, clarity of roles ...

'It creates an image, doesn't it?' says Smith. 'That's what we want in defence; we want to smother them and swarm them and destroy them. That's what the All Blacks are about – getting up and helping each other and smothering the opposition and giving them nothing.'

It's a visceral, visual metaphor that helped Smith turn his defensive vision into physical action, to 'operationalize' the purpose; to turn purpose into practice. It was easy to understand, to remember and apply under pressure, and it could be tailored across all aspects of training, briefing and even socializing.

Based in strong, resonant values, using a common language that employs mantras, mottos and metaphors, storytelling helps leaders connect their people's personal meaning to their vision of the future.

And it led to a World Cup.

~

The key criteria for creating a change story is fourfold.

○ The story must be credible and relevant – in Aristotelian poetics, it must have ethos (an authority and understanding of the subject) and logos (it must make rational sense).
○ It must be Visual and Visceral – appealing to the auditory,

visual and kinaesthetic receivers in our brains. It must seize our hearts as well as impress our heads. In terms of Aristotelian poetics, it must have pathos (it must be felt).

° It must be flexible and scaleable – as easily told around a campfire as across the boardroom table. This implies the use of simple, everyday language and ideas.

° And it must be useful – able to turn vision into action; purpose into practice – acting as a transferor of meaning between one domain and another, between 'your' world and 'mine', between the 'leader' and the 'led'.

Whether visual or verbal, motto, mantra or metaphor, language creates revolutions.

Invent Your Own Language

Strong cultures need a system of meaning understood by everyone, a language and vocabulary that binds the group together. This must have as its foundation the values of the group; in this way the story stays credible and relevant. Shrewd leaders invent a unique vocabulary as shorthand for communicating new cultural norms and standards, using specific words, phrases, mottos and mantras. Then, using metaphor, the leader begins to bring the story to visceral life across as many channels as possible. In this way, language becomes the oxygen that sustains belief. In this way, leaders rewrite the future.

Invent Your Own Language

Sing the world into existence.

He aha te kai o te rangatira. He kōrero, he kōrero, he kōrero.
What is the food of a leader? It is knowledge.
It is communication.

XIII

RITUAL

—— *'We're not all Māori. We're not all Polynesian . . .'*
Wayne Smith

RITUALIZE TO
ACTUALIZE
Create a culture

**New Zealand vs. South Africa, Carisbrook, Dunedin,
28 August 2005**

The anthems are over, the crowd quietens.

They know it is time.

The All Blacks cluster together, creating a wide scything arc across the field. A lone voice cries out.

It is Tana Umaga, the first Polynesian to captain New Zealand. A man of great *mana*.

Taringa whakarongo!

'Let your ears listen!'

In unison, his team crouches behind him. Umaga paces, his chest out, the silver fern, the black jersey, the chant continuing, momentum building.

Kia whakawhenua au i ahau!

'Let me become one with the land!'

The team join the challenge.

Ko Aotearoa e ngunguru nei!

'New Zealand is rumbling here.'

The team, advancing, advancing, stand tall and draw their thumbs across their throats.

A new *haka* is born. *'Kapa o Pango'*. A new legacy.

Au, au, aue hā!

It's our time! It's our moment!

And the All Blacks win, 31-27.

~

'People just don't realize how close we were to kicking the *haka* out completely,' says Gilbert Enoka. 'We were that close to losing the whole thing because we lost connection and understanding.' The senior players were saying, 'The TV cameras are shoved in our faces and all we want to do is get the thing over so we can play . . . and it's not for us, anyway, it's for the Māori people.'

'New Zealand society has changed,' says Graham Henry, 'it's not just Māori and European . . . the All Blacks team is made up of Tongan, Samoan, Fijian, European, Māori . . . and so the new *haka* encompasses the new culture and I think that is hugely important.'

'We would stand up and talk about Fijian culture,' he says, 'and talk about Samoan culture . . . we might have a Samoan meal after that talk.' It led to a 'greater understanding of the guys you are playing with' and a better understanding of 'New Zealand society'.

'They deconstructed it all,' says Anton Oliver. 'They asked, how are we going to create a legacy?'

'We had to manage the transition between Māori and Pacifica,' Enoka says. 'It wasn't until we sat down and said, tell us what it means to be a New Zealander and tell us what it means to be an All Black . . . then all of a sudden it came from a place inside them and had a connection and meaning and . . . the whole notion of your parents, your *tīpuna*, buried in the soil and you have a connection to the land and you put the jersey on and you've got a fern on and you're all connected.

'So all of a sudden your Fijians and the Tongans and the Samoans . . . could connect with the fact that, yes, this is our time, and this is our moment, and this is my time, and this is my moment.'

To help them in their quest, Henry, Smith, Hansen and Enoka brought in Derek Lardelli, a leading *tā moko* (Māori tattoo) artist, *kapa haka* (Māori dance) performer, cultural consultant, *tohunga* (wise man), teacher and artist.

He sat down with the leaders and began a conversation; a process of enquiry into the culture of the All Blacks, past and present. 'These conversations,' says Enoka, 'were the genesis of *Kapa o Pango*.'

'It was about 'using metaphors and multiple language', says Anton Oliver, 'and it was a huge renaissance. Massive. It was reconnecting with the Māori but it was actually even more reconnecting; it was actually reconnecting people from all different cultures into something, into one thing. The players could say, "I understand this. I made these words. These are my actions. It's my country. It's my land."'

And performance on the field of play? If you map the win/loss ratio against this newfound sense of collective identity, there's a direct and positive correlation.

Ritualize to actualize.

~

'Culture,' says Owen Eastwood, 'is like an organism, continually growing and changing.' Identity and purpose, he says, need to be continually renewed and reinterpreted to give them meaning. 'This cultural milieu is constantly changing,' agrees Anton Oliver. 'It's not a static thing.'

'Building trust, developing people and driving high-performance behaviours are never-ending tasks,' says Eastwood. 'Rituals are key for reinforcing the emotional glue.'

'It becomes absorbed,' says Enoka. 'Because with the power of the rituals, they're so strong, you don't have to spend two or three hours sitting in a room ...'

It's what Wayne Smith means when he talks about connecting to the central story, and what Enoka means by connecting to the core.

> Inspiring leaders establish rituals to connect their team to its core narrative, using them to reflect, remind, reinforce and reignite their collective identity and purpose.

'I think in the All Blacks' culture,' says Oliver, 'that's how it's passed on. So much of the legacy we have,' he says, 'is done through ritual.'

Ritualize to actualize.

~

Though the *haka* is the most famous, it is by no means the All Blacks' only ritual.

When Jonah Lomu received his first black jersey, it was handed to him by John Kirwan, an iconic predecessor in the same position.

'OK, you've made it,' said Sean Fitzpatrick, 'you're an All Black, enjoy it.'

'But,' added Kirwan, 'this is only the beginning. What you now have to do is be the best All Black ever to wear number 11.'

Ritualize to actualize.

When the All Blacks travel across the halfway point of the Severn Bridge on their way to play Wales, they stand up in the bus and shout, 'We never lose to Wales!' Once in Cardiff, the team will visit the Angel, the pub in which prop Keith Murdoch was involved in a scuffle that led to his being sent home in disgrace – he jumped the plane in Australia and disappeared into the Northern Territories, never to play rugby again. 'We have a beer to the fallen, right?' says Oliver. 'We lost one. We should never have lost one, it was ridiculous. So we pay recognition to him and what happened and the story gets passed on.'

The story gets passed on.

Meanwhile, there's a *tiki*, a carved Māori figure, buried on one corner of what was Cardiff Arms Park; there's the initiation ritual, flags on the wall, your place on the bus, anthems and caps, and a hundred other tiny rituals, some personal, some public: 'All these little things,' says Henry, 'they just add up and add to the *mana* of this group of people and their respect for each other and wanting to play for each other.'

Ritualize to actualize.

Rituals reflect, remind, reinforce and reignite the central story. They make it real in a vital, visceral way. From induction ceremonies to first caps, the *haka* to the hierarchies – they are the framework that holds the belief system in place. When the All Blacks perform the *haka* – or stand up on the bus to Wales and shout – they are connecting to something greater than themselves. They are making the metaphor their own, connecting their personal story to that of the team.

Sport, like business and diplomacy, is warfare by other means: a way for a band of 'warriors' to 'fight' for their side in 'battle' against an 'enemy'. So it's unsurprising that the All Blacks culture of ritualization, symbolism and narration is both relevant to business and also reflected in elite combat groups like the US Marine Corps.

Just as the All Blacks with its silver fern, the Marines have their 'Eagle, Globe and Anchor'. Just as the All Blacks say 'Once an All Black, always an All Black', so the Marines say, 'Once a Marine, always a Marine.' Just as the All Blacks have the Black Jersey, so the Marines have their Dress Blue. Both the Marines and the All Blacks 'improvise, adapt and overcome'. Both are the very best at what they do.

These rituals, symbols and mottos are the welt and weave of elite teams and organizations – the fabric that binds people together. Though the individuals change, the rituals remain, and these rituals are the structure that maintains belief.

Ritualize to actualize.

It need not be as obvious as a *haka*.

Opening an Apple product is a ritual, as is removing the

cigar band from a Montecristo. Whisky brands wrap their bottles in velvet. The Law Courts understand the implicit power of swearing on the Bible. We give gifts at Christmas.

It's not a coincidence that perhaps the most durable brand in the notoriously fly-by-night advertising business is Leo Burnett. The company's ritual began on the day it first opened for business – 5 August 1935, in the middle of the Great Depression. To brighten up an unfurnished reception area, someone put out a bowl of apples. The criticism wasn't long in coming.

'It won't be long,' a skeptical journalist wrote, 'until Leo Burnett is selling apples on the street corner instead of giving them away.'

In defiance – and in defence of fresh thinking – Leo Burnett has offered an apple to every visitor to the agency ever since and now gives away more than 1,000 apples around the world every day. And it has never had to sell them on street corners to survive.

Meanwhile, another agency, Saatchi & Saatchi, has its spirit statement, 'Nothing Is Impossible', embedded in the stone steps outside its office in Charlotte Street, London. It's another form of ritualization: when you enter the building you cross the threshold into a place where 'anything can happen'.

Something similar happens at Liverpool Football Club. As they walk to the pitch, both sides pass over the words 'This Is Anfield' inscribed on a sign – a ritual with different significance depending on the colour of your playing strip.

Rituals make beliefs real and tangible – they make them a 'thing'. They 'actualize'.

Take Lean Six Sigma, an efficiency improvements methodology. Central to its functioning is a belt-based training system: White, Yellow, Green, Black and Master Black Belts. This ritualization of process helps drive curiosity, concentration and internal competitiveness; reflecting, reminding, reinforcing and reigniting the purpose of the project.

Another, extraordinary, ritual is Wal-Mart's Saturday Morning Meeting, which has been going as long – fifty years – as the company itself. Now attended by thousands of employees, online and in person, it ritualizes knowledge sharing and collective endeavour. Guest speakers have included Bill Clinton, Warren Buffett, Henry Kissinger and Mark Zuckerberg.

Ritualize to actualize.

Rituals can be organizational: casual Fridays; drinks on a Friday night; the annual Christmas party.

They can be societal: red poppies, the giving of gifts or flowers, the wearing of diamonds, the invention of the word 'hello' to answer the phone; Christmas itself.

And they can be personal: former All Black Frank Bunce never let his jersey touch the floor, while another former All Black, Allan Hewson, wore the same pair of underpants for every test. After Neil Armstrong became the first man to walk on the moon, every time he glimpsed it in the night sky, he winked at it. At his funeral, instead accepting flowers or donations, his family asked the world to 'wink at the moon'.

Ritualize to actualize.

Large or small, formal or informal, corporate or creative, personal or professional – conscious or not – rituals continue to recreate meaning and have embedded within them the deep values and purpose of the person, the place or the project.

Though they often become almost invisible, they never lose

> Rituals tell your story, involve your people, create a legacy. Rituals make the intangible real.

their meaning, their metaphor, the story they tell us about ourselves and each other: that we're hospitable, collegiate, united, generous, respectful, remembering, reverent, committed or in love.

By inculcating rituals into a culture, leaders can bottle its essential spirit, capturing it for future generations. 'Tell me and I'll forget,' goes the old saying, 'show me and I may remember; involve me and I'll understand.'

Ritual represents a pre-verbal language, physicalizing experience. In combination with values and vocabulary, mantras and mottos, narratives and metaphors, signs and symbols, rituals achieve a literal embodiment through repetition of our central story. By enacting a ritual, we embody the belief system of our community and culture.

Ritual acts as a psychological process – a transition from one state into another. They take us into a new place of being.

A new being of team.

_____ *Ka tū te ihiihi*
We shall stand fearless
Ka tū te wanawana
We shall stand exalted in spirit
Ki runga ki te rangi
We shall climb to the heavens
E tū iho nei, tū iho nei, hī!
We shall attain the zenith, the utmost heights!
Au! Au! Au!

Ritualize to Actualize

The All Blacks are famous for their *haka*, one of the most exciting and distinctive phenomena in world sport. The crowds love it, as do the marketing people; it is central to the All Blacks' brand. Yet that is not why the team perform it. The All Blacks use the *haka* to reconnect with their fundamental purpose, to connect to the core of their culture, to summon their ancestors up from the earth to aid them in their battle, to intimidate the competition, and to bond with one another. Leaders can use rituals as a challenge to their opposition, and to themselves, to add to the legacy, to exceed expectations, to embody a belief system. By creating their own equivalent of the *haka*, leaders can attach a sense of personal meaning and belonging to the organization's overall purpose. Wise leaders look for ways to 'ritualize their enterprise', to find vivid, visceral processes that bring their ethos to life.

Ritualize to Actualize

Create a culture.

—— *Au, au, aue hā!*

It's our time! It's our moment!

XIV

WHAKAPAPA

_____ *E tāku mōkai, he wā poto noa koe i waenganui i te wā kua hipa me te wā kei tū mai.*
You are but a speck in the moment of time situated between two eternities, the past and the future.

BE A GOOD ANCESTOR
Plant trees you'll
never see

The Rope of Mankind

Gilbert Enoka is holding a long woven flax rope. It is a beautiful and mysterious thing, made by many hands in the traditional Māori manner and decorated at intervals by thin coloured ribbons. 'This is the flax the women of the land up on the East Coast went out and cut,' Enoka says. 'They boiled it and dried it and began to develop this rope.'

He points out the details. Three interwoven strands, black, silver and red, run its length in a long continuous spiral. *Te torino haere whakamua, whakamuri*, the proverb says. 'At the same time as the spiral is going forward, it is returning'. This rope, like many things within this extraordinary environment, is a metaphor for more than rugby. It stands for human life, our connection to our past, our present and our future.

'That's the silver fern of New Zealand,' Enoka says, pointing to a glistening strand. 'That's the blackness of our heritage and the jersey,' he adds, tracing another line down the length of the rope. 'And this represents the blood,' he says, pointing to the red strand. 'No matter if you are Samoan, Tokelauan, or anything, you're part of it, you have red blood. It weaves into the blackness.'

He points at the coloured strings: 'Each one a scalp,' he says. Blue for Argentina, crimson for Wales, a darker blue for France, and three red strings in a row. 'That was where we beat the British Lions . . .'

'When we lose,' he says, 'we put a black one on it. Because you've got to learn from it.'

'This would go up in every shed,' he says, hoisting the rope. 'It's about the rope and our connection with the rope. The idea is to bury this on Brian Lochore's farm. So that it goes back to the land.'

It is *Te Taura Tangata*, a Rope of Mankind.

It distills the ancestral soul of the team, connecting past, present and future, and stretches from the very beginning to the very end of time.

It is the *whakapapa* of a team.

Whakapapa is our genealogy – our place in the ascending order of all living things. Literally it means to pile rocks in layers, one upon the other, so that they reach from the earth to the heavens. It implies an eternal layering of our ancestors, our lives, our stories and myths, rising up from the beginning of time to this present moment and on into the future. It signifies the interdependence of everything – ancestry, spirituality, history, mythology and *mana* – all that is, all that has come before, all that will ever be. It is a fundamental tenet of the Māori people and the essential spirit of the All Blacks.

'To me, *whakapapa* is the highest expression of a team mindset,' says Owen Eastwood. 'I visualize this Māori idea as each of us being a link in an unbreakable chain of people, arm-in-arm, going back to when the tribe began – our first ancestor – through to the end of time. The sun slowly moves down this chain of people – signifying life.' He says that, 'What is important is that when the sun is on us we inherit our tribe's values, stories, mythology and standards – live to that standard – and then pass it on to the next person in the chain . . . I think this is the ultimate team mindset.'

In 1999, Adidas ran an advertisement which began with the oldest living All Blacks captain, Charlie Saxton, standing in an old locker room in his playing jersey. He pulls the jersey over his head and is 'reincarnated' as Fred Allen, the great All Blacks captain and coach. In chronological order successive jerseys reveal the string of captains through to Sean Fitzpatrick, and finally the then-All Blacks captain, Taine Randell.

It is a lineage of leadership.

'The legacy,' the super reads, 'is more intimidating than the opposition.'

'There's a big saying in the team,' Graham Henry says. '"You don't own the jersey, you're just the body in the jersey at the time." It's your job to continue the legacy and add to it when you get your opportunity. The current All Blacks team is playing for the guys that have played in the jersey before. That's hugely important to the current guys.'

> True leaders are stewards of the future. They take responsibility for adding to the legacy.

They also play for All Blacks yet to be born.

Fatherhood is an important theme within the All Blacks; this handing down of knowledge across the generations, this stewardship of the future.

'The reason your children turn out right is because their parents are right,' says Sean Fitzpatrick. 'The naughty little bastards are the ones where the parents are generally . . . it's a generalization, but are the ones that have been badly directed.'

'What you leave behind is not what is engraved in stone monuments, but what is woven into the lives of others.'

Ubuntu.

A dent in the universe.

In the All Blacks, in parenthood, in business, in life, it's about leaving the jersey in a better place. And it takes character.

~

'Never let the music die,' Jock Hobbs told the team at the start of the Rugby World Cup. Everyone in the room knew about his cancer, that it was terminal. But Hobbs wanted to pass some of the spirit on to a new generation. A few weeks later, he presented Richie McCaw with a silver cap marking his 100th Test as an All Black. Hobbs's legacy remains; his music hasn't died.

The music at the core of the All Blacks and all good leadership – that harmony of belief, pride, respect, humility, excellence, expectation, courage, purpose and sacrifice – is handed down from the past to the present, from the present to the future, in one long unbroken rope of life, an intellectual, emotional and spiritual *whakapapa*.

Toku toa, he toa rangatira, Māori say. My bravery is inherited from the chiefs who came before me. I stand tall on the shoulders of giants.

If we extrapolate that idea outward, into the world of desktops and cubicles, PowerPoint and deadlines, the idea of *whakapapa*, of legacy, of leaving the jersey in a better place, becomes a powerful leadership tool.

Boeing Commercial Airplanes, for instance, has a *whakapapa* that changed the world; from the 707 and the jet age, the 747 and mass long-haul tourism, the 737 and the short-haul budget airline, the 777 and the globalization of goods and passenger flight, and now with the 787, which despite teething problems is pioneering new frontiers in lower emission, high-efficiency flight, Boeing has put a dent in the universe. For those charged with developing the future of aviation, the legacy is more intimidating than the competition.

Similarly, Saatchi & Saatchi, in Kevin Roberts's words, is 'a legacy driven company'. From the outset they redefined the idea of an advertising agency and Roberts sees his role as continuing and enhancing that legacy. At Saatchi & Saatchi, as at Boeing, the legacy is more intimidating than the competition.

Similarly, Apple engineers wake up every morning to the

legacy of Steve Jobs, the iMac, iPod, iTunes, iPhone and iPad, and have to ask – what's next? And what's next after that? And what kind of ding can we put in the universe?

When you're known for changing the world one product at a time, these are compelling questions. But you don't need to be Boeing, or Saatchi & Saatchi, or Apple, or a team with a 75 per cent winning record over 100 years, to invoke the *whakapapa*.

In his remarkable essay, *Ancestors of the Mind*, Jim Traue discusses the idea of *whakapapa* from a Caucasian perspective, invoking the ideas handed down by literature as his intellectual and cultural lineage:

'Our ancestors of the mind include the great thinkers of Ancient Greece. The dramatists . . . the scientists . . . the mathematicians . . . the philosophers and moralists Socrates and Plato and Aristotle. All believed in the importance of ideas, the power of ideas, all believed that the highest purpose of humanity was to define the nature of truth, beauty, and justice.' You don't have to be an All Black, you don't have to be Māori, to understand that, as a leader, you can carry the ball forward and pass it on to the next generation.

Before Apple was 'Apple', Steve Jobs's hero was Dieter Rams at Braun. Compare Braun designs of the 1970s with contemporary Apple products to hear the music still playing. In the absence of a direct lineage, Jobs created one.

Meanwhile, Pixar's John Lassiter worshipped at the altar of Walt Disney and it is no coincidence that, in the end, the Disney Company bought up Pixar. Spiritually, they are soulmates. The music plays on.

Legacy begets legacies: that is their point and their power.

Equally, we all have our own individual *whakapapa*, the ancestral lineage that has brought us to our own moment in time. For each of us it is our moment, our time, our chance to shine.

'Life is no brief candle to me,' wrote George Bernard Shaw, 'It is a sort of splendid torch which I have got a hold of for the moment, and I want to make it burn as brightly as possible before handing it on to future generations.'

Don't let the music die.

Whakapapa is a primal human idea – somewhere between spiritual and philosophical, psychological and emotional – with great implications for the authentic leader.

It implies a stewardship of the past, reflected and reinvigorated through rituals and responsibilities – and a stewardship of the future. It is the kind of leadership that doesn't just valorize corporate boundaries, or shareholder value, or profit and loss columns, or ego, vanity and individual status. It cares instead about contribution to the lineage of the company and the team, even the planet – and about our contribution as individuals to a deeper continuum. It is a form of leadership that pays dividends in the same way as 'the score takes care of itself'.

And it delivers *mana*.

The true leader is called to 'leave the jersey in a better place', a code of conduct that aligns with Jonas Salk's belief that: 'our first responsibility is to be a good ancestor'.

~

Today it's hard for many of us to remember or imagine life as it was in the 1940s and 1950s.

Polio had reached epidemic proportions. Every parent's worst nightmare, it paralysed over 500,000 people around the world every year. The 'public reaction was to a plague,' wrote the US social historian William O'Neill. 'Citizens of urban areas were to be terrified every summer when this frightful visitor returned.' Sanatoria, callipers and withered limbs were embedded in the collective consciousness.

Jonas Salk changed all that. On 12 April 1955, he announced the Salk Vaccine, which relegated polio to a footnote of medical textbooks. It was hailed a miracle. Salk became a hero overnight, the most fêted man in America, yet he refused to patent his new vaccine, donating it to the human race instead.

'Example is not the main thing in influencing others,' said the philosopher Albert Schweitzer. 'It is the only thing.' Salk set a wise example. He used his fame to argue that it was time for the human race to change; consumerism, unfettered capitalism, environmental degradation and population growth is unsustainable, he argued, and it was our 'responsibility to find solutions to the key issues facing the human race'.

In his landmark book, *Survival of the Wisest*, he contends that mankind 'has not yet seen the importance of understanding life's "purpose", and therefore, his purpose individually and collectively, and of understanding where he fits into the evolutionary scheme of things.'

'What is my job on the planet? What is it that needs doing, that I know something about, that probably won't happen unless I take responsibility for it?'

As an Old Greek proverb tells us, 'A society grows great when old men plant trees whose shade they will never see'. While Better People Make Better All Blacks, they also make better scientists, CEOs, entrepreneurs, bankers, private equity investors, lawyers, advertising agency executives, butchers, bakers and candlestick makers. They make better mothers, fathers, sisters and brothers, better teachers, politicians and friends.

And together, collectively, incrementally, in a kind of compassionate *kaizen*, they make for a better world.

This is our social footprint.

Our social footprint is the impact our life has – or can have – on other lives. It begins with character – a deep respect for our deepest values - and it involves a committed enquiry into our life's purpose. What do we hold most sacred? What's our purpose here? What can we pass on, teach? What's our place in the *whakapapa*?

Great teams play with a higher purpose. From 'Uniting and Inspiring New Zealanders' to '*Ubuntu*', from '*Semper Fidelis*' to 'democratizing the automobile' to 'making the world a better place for everyone', to 'I have a Dream', the most inspiring leaders play a bigger, more important game.

Not so long ago, we respected bankers and hedge-fund financiers and vulture investors as though making money alone was enough. Patently – after the sleazy collapse of financial standards – this is not true anymore.

There is nothing wrong with making money but as a sole ambition it certainly isn't inspiring an emerging generation that values human connection, social interaction and authenticity more highly. In an increasingly secular Western world, people are looking for answers to the question that organized religion has provided for thousands of years: how to live. In an age of austerity, there is a desire for something that makes a lasting difference, a secular spirituality rather than evangelical materialism.

In a society badly let down by the promises of corporations, it seems that 'capitalism' has an opportunity to redefine itself and play a different game. It's not enough just to win anymore, we must win with flair. We must leave the jersey in a better place.

Fortunately for the more hard-headed businessperson, the result of this shift in approach is not just an altruistic fantasy or a meaningless sop to society. It is a very real driver for organizational performance, cohesion and conviction.

It is likely that the teams – whether companies or causes – that contribute a healthy social footprint will be those that survive and thrive over the coming decades. They'll recruit better talent, engender more loyalty and profit from a virtuous circle of purchase and recommendation, and build a sustainable culture of contribution and success. From their value to society will come their value as a company.

The cynics – those just in it for the money – have been found out. Theirs is no longer a sustainable model; increasingly, wealth on its own is no decent definition of success. It doesn't play well at dinner parties or in a eulogy.

By taking responsibility for something more than profits, we tap into a collective vibrancy that is not only good for the world but also good for business. To 'leave the jersey in a better place' means to work incrementally towards a better collective outcome. It means to be a custodian of the future, an architect of tomorrow, a steward of society. It means to live with respect, humility and excellence. It means *mana*.

As leaders it means that we will truly lead, not just manage, and that others will spill blood for our team. People want to believe in something bigger than themselves; purpose propels and moves people, and moving people is the purpose of a leader.

'Service to others,' said Muhammad Ali, 'is the rent you pay for your room here on earth.' But it's about more than rent, it's about respect: honouring that which we are capable of becoming, being great rather than just good, playing a bigger game, a more expansive game, a more ambitious game.

~

It all comes back to sweeping the sheds.

The word character comes from the Ancient Greek, *kharakter*, meaning the mark that is left on a coin during its manufacture. Character is also the mark left on you by life, and the mark we leave on life.

It's the impact you make when you're here, the trace you leave once you're gone.

Character rises out of our values, our purpose, the standards we set ourselves, our sacrifice and commitment, and the decisions we make under pressure, but it is primarily defined by the contribution we make, the responsibility we take, the leadership we show.

'Test rugby is all about testing your character,' says current All Blacks coach Steve Hansen. 'It's about putting you under pressure and seeing how you cope.'

John Wooden said, 'Be more concerned with your character than your reputation, because your character is what you really are, while your reputation is merely what others think you are.'

Character is forged by the way we respond to the challenges of life and business, by the way we lead our life and teams. If we value life, life values us. If we devalue it, we dishonour ourselves and our one chance at living. *This* is our time.

Leadership is surely the example we set. The way we lead our own life is what makes us a leader. It is what gives us *mana*.

Be a Good Ancestor

Our time is limited. Understanding the fragility of life is the first step in understanding our role and responsibility as a leader. Our greatest responsibility is to honour those who came before us and those who will come after, to 'leave the jersey in a better place'. We are the stewards of our organizations, the caretakers of our own lineage. Our actions today will echo beyond our time. They are our legacy. *Manaaki Whenua, Manaaki Tangata, Haere whakamua.* Care for the land, Care for the people, Go forward.

Be a Good Ancestor

Plant trees you'll never see.

_____ *E tipu, e rea, mō ngā rā o tōu ao.*

Grow and branch forth for the days of your world.

XV

LEGACY

——— *Te tōrino haere whakamua, whakamuri.*
At the same time as the spiral is going forward,
it is also returning.

WRITE YOUR LEGACY
This is your time

When a player makes the All Blacks, they're given a book. It's a small black book, bound in fine leather, and beautiful to hold.

The first page shows a jersey – that of the 1905 Originals, the team that began this long *whakapapa*. On the next page is another jersey, that of the 1924 Invincibles, and on the page after, another jersey, and another, and so on until the present day. It is a visual *whakapapa*, layered with meaning, a legacy to step into. The next few pages of this All Black handbook remind you of the principles, the heroes, the values, the standards, the code of honour, the ethos, the character of the team.

The rest of the pages are blank. Waiting to be filled.

It's time to make *your* mark, they say. *Your* contribution.

It's time to leave a legacy. *Your* legacy.

It's your time.

The First XV: Lessons in Leadership.

A rugby team has fifteen players who work together towards a common purpose, to win. These principles work in the same way. Each has a role, each a responsibility, each a position on the field. Combined they are the First XV.

I **Sweep the Sheds**
Never be too big to do the small
things that need to be done

II **Go for the Gap**
When you're on top of your game,
change your game

III **Play with Purpose**
Ask 'Why?'

IV **Pass the Ball**
Leaders create leaders

V **Create a Learning Environment**
Leaders are teachers

VI **No Dickheads**
Follow the spearhead

VII **Embrace Expectations**
Aim for the highest cloud

VIII **Train to Win**
Practise under pressure

IX **Keep a Blue Head**
Control your attention

X **Know Thyself**
Keep it real

XI **Sacrifice**
*Find something you would die for
and give your life to it*

XII **Invent a Language**
Sing your world into existence

XIII **Ritualize to Actualize**
Create a culture

XIV **Be a Good Ancestor**
Plant trees you'll never see

XV **Write Your Legacy**
This is your time

Whakataukī

_____ *Haere taka mua, taka muri; kaua e whai.*
Be a leader, not a follower.

_____ *Ehara taku toa i te toa takitahi, engari he toa takitini.*
Any success should not be attributed to me alone;
it was the work of us all.

_____ *Waiho mā te tangata e mihi.*
Let someone else praise your virtues.

_____ *Waiho kia pātai ana, he kaha ui te kaha.*
Let the questioning continue; the ability of the person
is in asking questions.

_____ *Kāore te kūmara e whāki ana tana reka.*
The kūmara (sweet potato) does not need to say
how sweet he is.

_____ *I orea te tuatara, ka puta ki waho.*
When poked at with a stick, the tuatara will emerge.
(A problem is solved by continuing to find solutions.)

_____ *He rangi tā Matawhāiti,*
he rangi tā Matawhānui.
The person with a narrow vision sees a narrow horizon,
the person with a wide vision sees a wide horizon.

_____ *Ki ngā whakaeke haumi.*
Join those who can join the sections of a canoe.
(Look for a leader who can bring people together.)

_____ *Kohia te kai rangatira, ruia te taitea.*
Gather the good food, cast away the rubbish.

_____ *Te tīmatanga o te mātauranga ko te wahangū,*
te wāhanga tuarua ko te whakarongo.
The first stage of learning is silence,
the second stage is listening.

_____ *Ā muri kia mau ki te kawau mārō, whanake ake,*
whanake ake.
Hold to the spearhead formation of the *kawau.*

_____ *He iti wai kōwhao waka e tahuri te waka.*
A little water seeping through a small hole may
swamp a canoe.

_____ *Kia urupū tātou; kaua e taukumekume.*
Let us be united, not pulling against one another.

_____ *Ko taku reo taku ohooho, ko taku reo taku māpihi mauria.*
My language is my awakening, my language is the
window to my soul.

_____ *Whāia te iti kahurangi; ki te tuohu koe,*
me he maunga teitei.
Aim for the highest cloud, so that if you miss it,
you will hit a lofty mountain.

———— *Ko te piko o te māhuri, tērā te tupu o te rākau.*
The way the sapling is shaped determines
how the tree grows.

———— *Tangata akona ki te kāinga, tūngia ki te marae,*
tau ana.
A person who is taught at home will stand
with confidence in the community.

———— *Mā te rongo, ka mōhio;*
Mā te mōhio, ka mārama;
Mā te mārama, ka mātau;
Mā te mātau, ka ora.
From listening comes knowledge;
From knowledge comes understanding;
From understanding comes wisdom;
From wisdom comes well-being.

———— *Whakapūpūtia mai ō mānuka, kia kore ai e whati.*
Cluster the branches of the manuka, so that they
will not break.

———— *He tangata kī tahi.*
A person who can be taken at his word.

———— *Ka tū te ihiihi*
Stand fearless

———— *Kaua e mate wheke, mate ururoa.*
Don't die like an octopus, die like a hammerhead shark.

_____ *Taringa whakarongo.*
Let your ears listen.

_____ *He aha te kai o te rangatira. He kōrero, he kōrero, he kōrero.*
What is the food of a leader? It is knowledge.
It is communication.

_____ *E tipu, e rea, mō ngā rā o tōu ao.*
Grow and branch forth for the days of your world.

_____ *Te tōrino haere whakamua, whakamuri.*
At the same time as the spiral is going forward,
it is also returning.

_____ *Manaaki Whenua, Manaaki Tangata, Haere whakamua.*
Care for the land, Care for the people, Go forward.

All Credit To

Thank you to Sir Graham Henry, Wayne Smith, Steve Hansen and Gilbert Enoka for your time and insights.

To Richie McCaw and his All Blacks – for welcoming me into your environment and for bringing the Webb Ellis Cup back where it belongs.

To Sean Fitzpatrick, Andrew Mehrtens and Anton Oliver for your time and for leaving the jersey in a better place.

To Steve Tew, Brian Finn, Darren Shand and Joe Locke for your professionalism and the unsung work you do behind the scenes for New Zealand rugby. To the engine room of the 2010 All Blacks – Dr Deb Robinson, Peter Gallagher, Nic Gill, Peter Duncan, Alistair Rogers, Mike Cron, Bianca Thiel, Grunta – and Poss. Thank you, and congratulations guys.

Kevin Chapman and Warren Adler, thank you for your faith – I hope we've left a legacy. George Kerr, for your acumen and support. Julie Helsen and Jan Clarke for the work you do with disadvantaged NZ children; you are heroes. To Nick Danziger, my wing man, for your talent and friendship.

Thank you also to Owen Eastwood of Hoko and Lewis Silkin, Will Hogg of Kinetic Consulting, Justin Hughes of Mission Excellence, Kevin Roberts of Saatchi & Saatchi, Paul Vaughan of Cardinal Red, Robbie Deans, Ken Franks, Bede Brosnahan of Gazing Performance Systems, and my colleagues and clients over the years for your business insights and support.

Thank you especially to Roger Hart, Ed Woodcock, Martin Grimer, Jim Paterson, Stephen Woodward and everyone at Aesop Agency for being 'the best storytelling agency in the world' and for your invaluable input, creativity and intelligence, particulary Dan Calderwood, for your design eye, and Fiona Chapman and Amy Loughnane for your eternal patience.

To the writers I've quoted, my special thanks. I'm all too aware I've clambered on the shoulders of giants in the making of this book and I hope I've done your ideas justice in such a short space. A special mention to Daniel Kahnemann, Daniel Pink, Victor Frankl, Bruce Chatwin, Stephen Sinek, Bob Howitt, Greg McGee, Matthew Syed, Bill Walsh, Jim Collins, John Wooden, Vince Lombardi, Phil Jackson, Pat Williams and Clive Woodward. Also, my thanks to Wynne Grey, Gregor Paul, Spiro Zavos, Pamela Hawley, Keith Quinn, David Benuik, Delice Coffey, Keith Rogers, Reg Birchfield, and all the other business and rugby journalists who have informed this work, and kept me informed.

And thank you to George Plimpton, whose *Paper Lion* started it all.

Thanks to Inia Maxwell, Kateia Burrows, Lauren Timihou-Farnsworth, and the staff at Te Puia, Rotorua, and also NZTC International for their help with the *whakataukī*. I'm keenly aware that I'm working with some sacred Māori beliefs and can only say that I do so with the utmost respect and reverence. My ancestors, too, are buried in *Aotearoa*.

Andreas Campomar, Charlotte Macdonald, Sam Evans, Rob Nichols and Clive Hebard at Constable & Robinson, thank you for supporting this idea and making it happen. Thanks to Fritha Saunders for your belief, Howard Watson for your concision and precision, and Pippa Masson, my agent, for your sage advice.

To Simon Coley and Jodi Redden, Sofia and Lu Lu, thank you for my home away from home in New Zealand – this book, these words, are not enough. Kristina Stoianova, Richard Boon, Cindy Baxter, Matthew and Ainsley Johnstone, Katherine Bonner, Keith Tannock, Andrew Donaldson, Sam Martin, Rob Kerr,

Jane Kerr, and Paul and Val Pelham – thank you. In your own ways you have helped make this project possible.

Sam and Charlie, my sons, thank you. You are my legacy.

Finally, my eternal gratitude to Holly.

For everything, for ever.

_____ *Ehara taku toa i te toa takitahi, engari he toa takitini.*

Any success should not be attributed to me alone;

it was the work of us all.

References

_____ *The greatest part of a writer's time is spent in reading. In order to write; a man will turn over half a library to make one book.*

Samuel Johnson, quoted in *The Life of Samuel Johnson* by James Boswell

Books

Armstrong, Alan, *Maori Games and Hakas* (Reed, 1964, reprinted 2005).

Broadwell, Paula and Vernon Loeb, *All In: The Education of General David Petraeus* (Penguin, 2012).

Brougham, A. E. and A. W. Reed, *Māori Proverbs* (A. H. & A. W. Reed, 1975).

Burke, Kenneth, *The Philosophy of Literary Form: Studies in Symbolic Action* (University of California Press, 1974).

Calne, Donald, *Within Reason: Rationality and Human Behaviour* (Pantheon Books, 1999).

Campbell, Joseph, *Myths to Live By* (Viking Press, 1972).

Campbell, Joseph with Bill Moyers, *The Power of Myth* (Doubleday, 1988).

Carlson, Anthony, Donald P. Wright Michael Doidge, *Thunder Run, a case study in Misssion Command, Baghdad* (Combat Studies Institute Press, iBook, 2013).

Chandler, Alfred Dupont, *Strategy & Structure: Chapters in the History of the Industrial Enterprise* (MIT Press, 1962).

Chatwin, Bruce, *The Songlines* (Vintage Classics, 1986).

Cochrane, Brett and James Kerr, *Twenty Eight Heroes* (Teddy Bears Press, 1991).

Codrington, Robert, *The Melanesian Languages* (Clarendon Press, 1885).

Collins, Jim, *Good to Great* (Random House, 2001).

Covey, Stephen R., *The 7 Habits of Highly Effective People* (Simon & Schuster, 2004).

Feinstein, John, *A Season on the Brink* (Fireside, 1986).

Fitzpatrick, Sean and Andrew Fitzgerald, *Winning Matters: Being the Best You Can Be* (Penguin, 2011).

Frankl, Victor E., *Man's Search for Meaning* (Ebury, 2004).

George, Bill, *True North: Discover Your Authentic Leadership* (Jossey Bass, 2007).

Gilson, Clive, Mike Pratt, Kevin Roberts and Ed Weymes, *Peak Performance: Business Lessons from the World's Top Sports Organizations* (HarperCollins, 2001).

Goethals, George, Georgina Sorenson and James MacGregor Burns, *Encyclopedia of Leadership* (Sage, 2004).

Handy, Charles, *Empty Raincoat: Making Sense of the Future* (Arrow, 2002).

Hite, J. *Learning in Chaos* (Gulf Publishing Company, 1999).

Howitt, Bob, *Graham Henry: Final Word* (HarperCollins, 2012).

Isaacson, Walter, *Steve Jobs: The Exclusive Biography* (Little, Brown, 2011).

Jackson, Phil and Hugh Delehanty, *Sacred Hoops* (Hyperion, 1995).

Kahneman, Daniel, *Thinking, Fast and Slow* (Farrar, Strauss and Giroux, 2011).

Kerr, James and Nick Danziger, *Mana* (Hachette, 2010).

Kipling, Rudyard, *The Second Jungle Book*.

Kotter, John, *Leading Change: An Action Plan from the World's Foremost Expert on Business Leadership* (Harvard Business Press, 1996).

Lombardi Jr. Vince, *The Lombardi Rules* (McGraw-Hill, 2003).

Longworth, Philip, *The Art of Victory* (Holt, Rinehart, and Winston, 1965).

McCaw, Richie with Greg McGee, *The Real McCaw* (Hachette NZ, 2012).

McConnell, Robin, *Inside the All Blacks* (HarperCollins, 1998).

Masaaki, Imai, *Kaizen: The Key to Japan's Competitive Success* (Random House, 1986).

Moko Mead, Hirini & Grove, Neil, *Ngā Pēpeha a ngā Tīpuna (The Sayings of the Ancestors)* (Victoria University Press, 2001).

Moore, Richard, *Sky's Limit: Wiggins & Cavindish: The Quest to Conquer the Tour de France* (Harper Sport, 2011).

Patterson, Kerry, Grenny, Joseph, Maxfield, David, McMillan, Ron and Switzler, Al, *Influencer: The Power to Change Anything* (McGraw-Hill, 2008).

Peters, Tom, *Thriving on Chaos* (HarperBusiness, 1989).

Peters, Tom and Robert H. Waterman, Jr., *In Search of Excellence: Lessons from America's Best-Run Companies* (Harper Business, 1992).

Pink, Daniel L., *Drive: The Surprising Truth about What Motivates Us* (Canongate, 2011).

Plimpton, George, *Paper Lion* (Harper & Row, 1965).

Richards, Ellen, *Euthenics: The Science of Controllable Environment: A Plea for Better Conditions As a First Step Toward Higher Human Efficiency* (Whitcomb & Barrows, 1912).

Salk, Jonas, *Survival of the Wisest* (Harper & Row, 1973).

Sartre, Jean-Paul, *Essays in Existentialism* (Citadel Press, 1967).

Schwarzenegger, Arnold, *Total Recall: My Unbelievable True Life Story* (Simon & Schuster, 2012).

Sinek, Simon, *Start with Why: How Great Leaders Inspire Everyone to Take Action* (Penguin, 2009).

Stone, W. Clement and Napoleon Hill, *Success Through a Positive Mental Attitude* (Prentice-Hall, 1960).

Suvorov, Alexander Vasilyevich, *The Science of Victory* (1776).

Suzuki, Shunryu, *Zen Mind, Beginner's Mind* (Shambhala, 2011).

Syed, Matthew, *Bounce: The Myth of Talent and the Power of Practice* (HarperCollins, 2010).

Te Taiao: Māori and the Natural World (Bateman, 2010).

Thompson, Jeffrey, *Flicker to Flame; Living with Purpose, Meaning and Happiness* (Parker, 2006).

Thucydides, *History of the Peloponnesian War*, 11.43.

Tozawa, Bunji and Norman Bodek, *The Idea Generator: Quick and Easy Kaizen* (PCS Press, 2001).

Traue. J. E., *Ancestors of the Mind: A Pakeha Whakapapa* (Gondwanaland Press, 1990).

Tu, Khoi, *Superteams: The Secrets of Stellar Performance from Seven Legendary Teams* (Penguin, 2012).

Tutu, Bishop Desmond, *No Future Without Foregiveness* (Image, 2000).

Ulrich, David, *Delivering Results: A New Mandate for Human Resource Professionals* (Harvard Business School Press, 1991).

US Department of Defense, *Dictionary of Military and Associated Terms* (US Department of Defense, 2013), available at www.dtic.mil/doctrine/dod_dictionary.

Verdon, Paul, *Tribute* (Cumulus, 2001).

Walsh, Bill with Jamison, Steve and Walsh, Craig, *The Score Takes Care of Itself: My Philosophy of Leadership* (Penguin, 2009).

Wolfe, Tom, *The Electric Kool Aid Acid Test* (Picador, 2008).

Wooden, John and Steve Jamison, *The Wisdom of Wooden: My Century On and Off the Court* (McGraw-Hill, 2010).

— *Wooden: A Lifetime of Observations and Reflections On and Off the Court* (McGraw-Hill, 1997).

Zaffron, Steve and Logan, Dave, *The Three Laws of Performance: Rewriting the Future of Your Organization and Your Life* (John Wiley & Sons, 2011).

Essays/Papers/Articles

Alderson, Andrew; *Rugby: Chiefs riding a surging tide in title defence bid*; http://www.nzherald.co.nz/sport/news/article. cfm?c_id=4&objectid=10863073

Ashton, Brian, *All Blacks Red/Blue Thinking Lights: A Path Everyone Else Should Follow,* available at www.independent. co.uk/sport/rugby/rugby-union/news-comment/brian-ashton-all-blacks-redblue-thinking-lights-a-path-everyone-else-should-follow-6257512.html *(2011).*

Bargh, John A; Chen, Mark; Burrows, Lara; *Automaticity of Social Behaviour: Direct effects of trait construct and stereotype activation on action,* (Journal of Personality and Social Pyschology, 1996).

Boyd, John R., *'Destruction and Creation'*, US Army Command and General Staff College (1976), available at www. goalsys.com/books/documents/destruction_and_creation.pdf.

Cleaver, Dylan, *The stuff of champions: Dan Carter*, (New Zealand Herald, 2012).

Collins, Tom, *Mythic Reflections: Thoughts on Myth, Spirit, and Our Times: An Interview With Joseph Campbell,* The New Story (Contect Institute 1985/86).

Dempsey, General Martin E., *'America's Military: A Profession of Arms'*, US Department of Defense (2012), available at www.defense.gov/news/newsarticle.aspx?id=67303.

Erhard, Werner, Jensen, Michael C. and Zaffron, Steve, *'Integrity: Where Leadership Begins – A New Model of Integrity'*, Barbados Working Paper/Harvard Business School NOM Working Paper No. 07-03 (2007), available at papers.ssrn.com/sol3/papers.cfm?abstract_id=983401.

Hawley, Pamela, http://pamelahawley.wordpress. com/2013/01/18/the-self-esteem-of-leadership/

Department of the Army headquarters, http://www.bits.
de/NRANEU/others/amd-us-archive/fm6(03).pdf/ Mission
Command: Command and Control of Army Forces/ (2003).

Henry, Graham, therugbysite.com/blog-posts/66/-my-
most-important-lesson-by-graham-henry

Jensen, Michael C, *'Integrity: Without It Nothing Works'*,
Rotman Magazine: The Magazine of the Rotman School of
Management (Fall 2009), Barbados Working Paper No. 09-04/
Harvard Business School NOM Working Paper No. 10-042 (2007),
available at papers.ssrn.com/sol3/papers.cfm?abstract_id=1511274.

Kasekove, Evan, *The Legacy of Bob Knight* (The Muhlen-
berg Weekly, 2011).

Kotter, John, *The Power of Stories*, (www.forbes.com/2006/
04/12/power-of-stories-oped-cx_jk_01412kotter.html)

Luck, General (Retired) Gary and the JS j7 Deployable
Training Division, *Insights and best practices paper; Mission
Command and Cross-Domain Synergy*, (http://www.dtic.mil/
doctrine/fp/mission_command_fp.pdf, published under the sus-
pices of Joint Staff J7, March 2013).

McKendry, Patrick, *All Blacks; Preparation is the Key*,
(NZ Herald, 2012).

Maslow, Abraham, *'A Theory of Human Motivation'*,
Psychological Review, 50 (1943).

Paul, Gregor, nzrugbyworld.co.nz/features1154/mind-games

Paul, Gregor, *The All Blacks' longest night heralded a new
dawn* (New Zealand Herald, 2012).

Reason, Mark, *The Voice of Reason* (www. therugbysite.
com/blog-posts/305-what-stuart-lancaster-can-really-learn-
from-bill-walsh-by-mark-reason)

Rich, Dr Judith, www.huffingtonpost.com/dr-judith-rich-/ubuntu_b_1834779.html. Transcription of Nelson Mandela in interview with Tim Modise.

Rogers, Keith, www.reviewjournal.com/news/lasvegas/air-force-helping-hone-new-corps-leaders-2011

Rose DR, 'Fact Sheet – Polio Vaccine Field Trial of 1954' (March of Dimes Archives, 2004 02 11).

Rutledge, Dr Pamela, *Transmedia Storytelling: The Pyschological Power of Story* (mprcenter.org/blog/pamela-rutledge, 2011).

Slater, Matt, bbc.co.uk/sport/o/olympics/19174302

Sheringham, Sam, bbc.co.uk/blogs/sam-sherigham/2012/06/tino-best-from-the-ridiculous.html

Tozawa, Bunji; *The improvement engine: creativity & innovation through employee involvement: the Kaizen teian system.* Japan Human Relations Association (1995). Productivity Press. pp. 34. ISBN 9781563270109.

Films

Training with the Forwards: Brad Thorn, Whero Films
www.youtube.com/watch?v=VOS5O0-RItM

    Inside the Black Jersey; Chapter Four: The Coaches;
www.youtube.com/watch?v=agJMEP_C2kQ

Websites

www.bbc.co.uk/news

www.billgeorge.org

www.coachwooden.com

www.chalkprojects.com

www.fastcompany.com

www.frontrowgroup.co.uk

www.gazing.com

www.hbr.org

www.independent.co.uk

www.inthewinningzone.com

www.krconnect.blogspot.com

leadershipconference.wharton.upenn.edu

www.londonbusinessforum.com

www.management.co.nz

www.nature.com

www.newsroom.ucla.edu

news.stanford.edu/news/2005/june5/jobs-0161505.html

www.nzherald.com

www.rebonline.com.au/people/4838-leader-mind-games. 2012

www.reviewjournal.com

www.sportspsychologybasketball.com

www.teara.govt.nz

www.telegraph.co.uk

www.theroar.com.au

www.therugbysite.com

Lyrics/Dialogue

Any Given Sunday, screenplay by John Logan and Oliver Stone, directed by Oliver Stone, Warner Bros, Ixtlan, Donner's Company (1999).

The *haka*, *Ka Mate*, was written by Te Rauparaha of Ngäti Toa.

Kapa o Pango was developed by the All Blacks with Derek Lardelli of Ngāti Porou using some lyrics of *No Niu Tirini*, the *haka* used by the 1924 All Blacks and descended from that of the earthquake God, Raumoko, *Ko Ruaumoko e ngungurunei*.

The phrases 'barefoot guru', 'cups of carbohydrates' and 'huge schoolboys' refer to *Twenty Eight Heroes* by Cochrane and Kerr.

Interviews

Sir Graham Henry, Wayne Smith, Gilbert Enoka, Sean Fitzpatrick, Andrew Mehrtens, Anton Oliver, Owen Eastwood, Kevin Roberts, Will Hogg, Ed Woodcock, Roger Hart, Justin Hughes, Ken Franks, Bede Brosnahan, Richie McCaw and the 2010 All Blacks.

Special thanks to Bede Brosnahan and Gazing Performance Systems for their input on training with intensity and performing under pressure. Special thanks also to Will Hogg and Kinetic Consulting for input on culture change and engagement. Special thanks to Greg McKee, most especially for the Uncle Bigsy story in *The Real McCaw*, Bob Howitt for the invaluble background for the culture change sections, Gregor Paul for his work looking into the 'mind game', and Owen Eastwood for his insights on culture and competitive advantage. Special thanks also to Roger Hart, Ed Woodcock and Aesop Agency for their insights and input on brand storytelling.

You can find the author at www.chalkprojects.com

For Jo Jo
All who came before her,
and all who will come after.

—— *Kua hinga te tōtara haemata i te wao nui a Tāne.*
A mighty tree has fallen in the forest of Tāne.